31

At Issue

Ethanol

Other Books in the At Issue Series:

At Issue

Ethanol

Suzanne Dewsbury and Ian M. Dewsbury, Book Editors

GREENHAVEN PRESS
A part of Gale, Cengage Learning

GALE
CENGAGE Learning™

Detroit • New York • San Francisco • New Haven, Conn • Waterville, Maine • London

GALE
CENGAGE Learning

Christine Nasso, *Publisher*
Elizabeth Des Chenes, *Managing Editor*

© 2009 Greenhaven Press, a part of Gale, Cengage Learning.

Gale and Greenhaven Press are registered trademarks used herein under license.

For more information, contact:
Greenhaven Press
27500 Drake Rd.
Farmington Hills, MI 48331-3535
Or you can visit our Internet site at gale.cengage.com

For product information and technology assistance, contact us at

Gale Customer Support, 1-800-877-4253
For permission to use material from this text or product, submit all requests online at www.cengage.com/permissions

Further permissions questions can be emailed to permissionrequest@cengage.com

Articles in Greenhaven Press anthologies are often edited for length to meet page requirements. In addition, original titles of these works are changed to clearly present the main thesis and to explicitly indicate the author's opinion. Every effort is made to ensure that Greenhaven Press accurately reflects the original intent of the authors. Every effort has been made to trace the owners of copyrighted material.

Cover photograph copyright, Debra Hughes 2007. Used under license from Shutterstock-.com.

LIBRARY OF CONGRESS CATALOGING-IN-PUBLICATION DATA

Ethanol / Suzanne Dewsbury and Ian M. Dewsbury, book editors.
    p. cm. -- (At issue)
  Includes bibliographical references and index.
  ISBN 978-0-7377-4414-9 (hardcover)
  ISBN 978-0-7377-4415-6 (pbk.)
  1. Alcohol as fuel. I. Dewsbury, Suzanne. II. Dewsbury, Ian M.
  TP358.E78 2009
  333.95'39--dc22

                                                2008052824

Printed in the United States of America
1 2 3 4 5 6 7 13 12 11 10 09

Contents

Introduction

On August 8, 2005, President George W. Bush signed into law the Energy Policy Act of 2005, a comprehensive energy bill that included a renewable-fuel standard, which was expected to double the use of ethanol and biodiesel as alternative motor vehicle fuels in the United States by 2012. In his 2007 State of the Union address, the president called for the passage of additional mandates requiring the use of 35 billion gallons of renewable and alternative fuels by 2017, five times the 2012 levels required in the Energy Policy Act. Partly as a result of this legislation, America's ethanol production capacity grew from 1.9 billion gallons in 2001 to 6.1 billion gallons in 2007. Along with this rise in production, ethanol has become the topic of much public debate, and the disagreement between proponents and detractors shows no signs of being resolved in the near future.

Under current government policy, nearly every stage of ethanol production is subsidized in some way by federal, state, or local government. A report prepared for the International Institute for Sustainable Development estimated the total cost of ethanol subsidies in the United States for 2006 at between $5.1 and $6.8 billion. The study noted that while the total cost of subsidization for ethanol was still below the total cost for conventional fuels such as petroleum products and energy from nuclear fission, when measured in terms of cost of the subsidy per unit of energy supplied, liquid biofuels (including ethanol) enjoy a level of subsidization "close to the top for all energy sources."

Given the massive extent of public expenditure, the central question of the ethanol debate must be "Is it worth it?" To answer this question, ideally we would have a balance sheet totaling all the benefits of increased ethanol use in one column, and all the costs in another. Then, simply by comparing the columns, we could reach a decision as to whether our current policy is wise. However, in the case of ethanol, much of the disagreement concerns what exactly should be counted as a benefit or a cost. Indeed, simply by expanding or narrowing the focus of our analysis—by including more or less within the realm of potential costs and benefits—we can come to quite different answers to the question "Is it worth it?" And, of course, there is disagreement as to whether any particular consequence of rising ethanol use should be considered beneficial, detrimental, or irrelevant.

As an example of proponents and detractors focusing their arguments at a different level, take the current controversy over the effect of ethanol use on the price of food. Because nearly all of the ethanol currently produced in the United States is made from corn, the more ethanol we produce, the less corn we have available to use as food. By the law of supply and demand, this would be expected to drive up the cost of food that contains corn or uses corn in its production. The latter category includes most meat, since corn is a major component of agricultural feed. Proponents of ethanol point out that even as corn prices have reached record highs, the retail price of food in the United States has gone up by only a small amount. Furthermore, the increase in food prices that has been observed can also be explained by a rise in oil prices, which drives up the cost of producing and transporting food.

Ethanol's detractors, however, are quick to point out that the United States is the world's largest exporter of cereal grains, including corn. The costs of American ethanol use, they argue, are felt most acutely by those who live in the poorest countries in the world. It is certainly true that food prices have gone up most dramatically in developing countries that are net importers of food. Mexico, for example, has seen public riots over the rapidly rising cost of tortillas made from corn. So, the proponents of ethanol may be right that U.S. food prices do not change much in relation to the wholesale price of corn, while, at the same time, detractors of ethanol may be right that worldwide food prices are rising dramatically as a result of American ethanol policies. The difference, again, is one of focus.

As mentioned above, there also may be disagreement over whether a particular effect of ethanol use should be considered beneficial or detrimental. For example, there is no doubt that the rise in corn prices due to increased demand for ethanol has been good for those who grow corn. Proponents of ethanol point out that the ethanol boom has been largely responsible for an economic resurgence in many rural communities that, until recently, had experienced steady decline. They obviously see this as a good thing. Some of ethanol's detractors, on the other hand, point out that the primary beneficiary is not necessarily the iconic American farmer, but rather the owner of agricultural land—often a large corporation or absentee landlord. On this account, policies encouraging ethanol amount to no more than taking money away from taxpayers in general and giving it to these landowners. In contrast to ethanol's proponents, the detractors obviously see this as a bad thing.

These few examples serve to illustrate the ways in which those concerned with ethanol policy may disagree not only on the proper conclusions to be drawn given the evidence available, but on what evidence should be considered in the first place and on the very terms of the debate. The dramatic rise in world oil prices in 2008—along with growing concern that the funds we use to pay for oil from foreign sources amounts to a vast transfer of wealth from America to countries that may not be our allies in the war on terror—have served to render the ethanol debate at once more complicated and more vital.

1

Ethanol: An Overview

American Coalition for Ethanol

The American Coalition for Ethanol is a nonprofit organization whose membership includes farmers, ethanol producers, and investors in the ethanol industry. The organization supports the increased production and use of ethanol in America and publishes an online magazine at www.ethanoltoday.com.

Ethanol, a renewable fuel produced from agricultural products such as corn, can be blended in various proportions with ordinary gasoline. The two most common blends are E10, which is 10 percent ethanol and 90 percent gasoline, and E85, which is 85 percent ethanol and 15 percent gasoline. While E10 can be used in all types of automobiles, E85 can be used only in "flexible fuel" vehicles. The use of ethanol in gasoline has many benefits, including cleaner auto emissions and a boost to local economies where corn for ethanol is grown and where ethanol is refined. In addition, because ethanol is domestically produced, it helps to reduce America's dependence on foreign sources of petroleum.

Ethanol is a clean-burning, high-octane motor fuel that is produced from renewable sources. At its most basic, ethanol is grain alcohol, produced from crops such as corn. Because it is domestically produced, ethanol helps reduce America's dependence upon foreign sources of energy.

Pure, 100% ethanol is not generally used as a motor fuel; instead, a percentage of ethanol is combined with unleaded

American Coalition for Ethanol, "Ethanol 101," accessed June 7, 2008. Reproduced by permission. http://www.ethanol.org.

gasoline. This is beneficial because the ethanol decreases the fuel's cost, increases the fuel's octane rating, and decreases gasoline's harmful emissions.

Any amount of ethanol can be combined with gasoline, but the most common blends are:

E10—10% ethanol and 90% unleaded gasoline. E10 is approved for use in any make or model of vehicle sold in the U.S. Many automakers recommend its use because of its high performance, clean-burning characteristics. Today about 46% of America's gasoline contains some ethanol, most as this E10 blend.

E85—85% ethanol and 15% unleaded gasoline. E85 is an alternative fuel for use in flexible fuel vehicles (FFVs). There are currently more than 6 million FFVs on America's roads today, and automakers are rolling out more each year. In conjunction with more flexible fuel vehicles, more E85 pumps are being installed across the country. When E85 is not available, these FFVs can operate on straight gasoline or any ethanol blend up to 85%.

If . . . higher percentages of ethanol could be used in standard automobiles, the U.S. could use a dramatically higher amount of renewable fuel, thus significantly decreasing our dependence on petroleum.

It is important to note that it does not take a special vehicle to run on "ethanol." All vehicles are "ethanol vehicles" and can use up to 10% ethanol with no modifications to the engine. Often people confuse E85 for "ethanol," believing incorrectly that not all vehicles are ethanol compatible.

Mid-range blends of ethanol: between E10 and E85. ACE [American Coalition for Ethanol] is leading efforts to attend to any technical or regulatory hurdles to using ethanol blends above 10%, such as E20, E30, or E40. If these higher percentages of ethanol could be used in standard automobiles, the

U.S. could use a dramatically higher amount of renewable fuel, thus significantly decreasing our dependence on petroleum.

New research shows that mid-range ethanol blends can in some cases provide better fuel economy than regular unleaded gasoline—even in standard non-flex-fuel vehicles. Previous assumptions that ethanol's lower energy content directly correlates with lower fuel economy were found to be incorrect. Instead, the research suggests there is an "optimal blend level" of ethanol and gasoline (most likely E20 or E30) at which vehicles will get better mileage than predicted based on the fuel's per-gallon Btu [British thermal unit, an energy measurement] content.

ACE has also collaborated on research to examine the impact of using higher blends of ethanol in standard automobiles. A non flex-fuel 2001 Chevrolet Tahoe, which had traveled more than 100,000 miles almost exclusively on E85, was donated to research and was torn down to examine the fuel's impact on the engine components.

Benefits of Ethanol

Economy and Job Creation Benefits. The production and use of ethanol benefits our economy on all levels—local, state, and national. From the local communities where the crops are grown and processed to the metropolitan areas where drivers fill up with a domestically produced fuel, American-made ethanol propels the economy.

In its 2002 study "Ethanol and the Local Community," AUS Consultants and SJH & Company found that:

- With an approximate cost of $60 million for one year of construction, an ethanol plant expands the local economic base by $110 million each year.

- Ethanol production will generate an additional $19.6 million in household income annually.

- Tax revenue for local and state governments will increase by at least $1.2 million a year.

- Nearly 700 permanent jobs will be created in the area near an ethanol plant.

Agriculture, Farmers, and Rural Communities. Ethanol production and use benefit U.S. agriculture and lead rural economic development. Because it is made primarily from corn and other agricultural products, ethanol increases demand for these crops, increases the prices farmers receive for these crops, and brings economic development opportunity to the rural areas where the ethanol is made.

American-made, renewable ethanol directly displaces crude oil we would need to import, offering our country critically needed independence and security from foreign sources of energy.

Over the past decade, farmer-owned and locally-owned ethanol plants have driven the dramatic growth in the U.S. ethanol industry. Of the nation's total ethanol production capacity, about 40% is owned and controlled by U.S. farmers and other local investors. This represents the largest single ownership category in the industry.

The U.S. ethanol industry has increased demand for corn and has played a role in bolstering chronically low corn prices, allowing farmers to earn a modest, market-based profit on their crop. Studies have shown that the local price of corn increases by at least 5–10 cents per bushel in the area around an ethanol plant, adding significantly to the farm income in the area.

USDA [U.S. Department of Agriculture] estimates that the Renewable Fuel Standard [part of the Energy Policy Act of 2005] will generate an additional $2 billion to $4 billion in net farm income by 2012.

Energy Security and Independence. American-made, renewable ethanol directly displaces crude oil we would need to import, offering our country critically needed independence and security from foreign sources of energy.

Current U.S. ethanol production capacity of 6 billion gallons per year can reduce gasoline imports by more than one-third and effectively extends gasoline supplies at a time when refining capacity is at its maximum.

Ethanol reduces harmful tailpipe emissions of carbon monoxide, particulate matter, oxides of nitrogen, and other ozone-forming pollutants.

According to the Energy Information Administration, the 7.5 billion gallon ethanol production level minimum set in the Renewable Fuels Standard could reduce oil consumption by 80,000 barrels per day.

Ethanol is key to reducing our country's trade deficit in crude oil, a figure that has been steadily increasing: $27 billion in 1987 up to $100 billion in 2002. The U.S. Commerce Department estimates that each $1 billion of trade deficit costs the U.S. 19,100 jobs.

Energy Independence Facts:

- The U.S. imports about two-thirds of its oil, and some experts predict our dependence upon foreign crude could climb to 70% in the years to come.

- For every barrel of ethanol produced (1 barrel = 42 gallons), 1.2 barrels of petroleum are displaced at the refinery. (Information Resources Inc.)

- In addition to importing record amounts of oil, the U.S. has also been importing record amounts of finished gasoline: 37 million gallons per day. (Energy Information Administration)

- U.S. fuel consumption increased from 12 billion gallons per year in 1970, to 160 billion gallons in 2002. (Federal Highway Administration)

Environment and Clean Air. Fossil fuel-based gasoline is the largest source of man-made carcinogens and the number one source of toxic emissions, according to the U.S. EPA [Environmental Protection Agency]. Ethanol is a renewable, environmentally friendly fuel that is inherently cleaner than gasoline. Ethanol reduces harmful tailpipe emissions of carbon monoxide, particulate matter, oxides of nitrogen, and other ozone-forming pollutants.

The use of ethanol-blended fuel helps reduce the environmental and economic impacts of gasoline consumption on our society.

Ethanol Clean Air Facts:

- Ethanol blends are likely to reduce carbon monoxide emissions in vehicles by between 10%–30%, depending upon the combustion technology. (U.S. EPA)

- The American Lung Association of Metropolitan Chicago credits ethanol-blended fuel with reducing smog-forming emissions by 25% since 1990.

- The use of 10% ethanol blends reduces greenhouse gas emissions by 12%–19% compared to conventional gasoline. (Argonne National Lab)

- In 2004, ethanol use in the U.S. reduced CO2-equivalent greenhouse gas emissions by approximately 7 million tons, equal to removing the emissions of more than 1 million cars from the road. (Argonne National Lab)

- Research shows a 35%–46% reduction in greenhouse gas emissions and a 50%–60% reduction in fossil energy use due to the use of ethanol as a motor fuel. (Argonne National Lab)

- Ethanol contains 35% oxygen, making it burn more cleanly and completely than gasoline.

- E85 has the highest oxygen content of any fuel available, making it burn even more cleanly and even more completely than any other fuel.

- E85 contains 80% fewer gum-forming compounds than gasoline.

- Ethanol is highly biodegradable, making it safer for the environment.

2

Producing Ethanol from Corn Is Energy Efficient

David Morris

David Morris is vice president of the Institute for Local Self-Reliance and author of Ethanol Policy and Development: 1978–1992, The Carbohydrate Economy: Making Chemicals and Industrial Materials from Plant Matter, *and* How Much Energy Does It Take to Make a Gallon of Ethanol? *He has served as an advisor or consultant to the energy departments of Presidents Gerald Ford, Jimmy Carter, Bill Clinton, and George W. Bush and currently serves on the advisory committee to the United States Department of Agriculture and Department of Energy on biomass and biofuels.*

There are a number of problems with studies claiming a negative net energy balance for ethanol produced from corn. Perhaps the most important problem is that these studies rely on outdated data on farming methods and ethanol production. Today's farming practices and ethanol plants are much more efficient than those of 20 years ago, and the studies fail to account for this. Furthermore, the studies assume that the question of net energy balance is the most important one facing policy makers. The quality of ethanol as a fuel, its benefits in terms of environmental impact, and the value of reducing dependence on petroleum should also be taken into consideration.

Among the many environmental factors to consider [with regard to ethanol and other biofuels] is that of energy balance, that is, the amount of energy it takes to grow a crop and convert it into biofuels and other products compared to the amount of energy contained in the resulting biofuel and bioproducts.

Net energy is an issue worthy of investigation. Unfortunately, this small piece of the puzzle has tended to dominate the discussion of biofuels. In the process, important issues like the ownership structure of a carbohydrate economy or its implications for world trade and rural development have largely been ignored.

Instead of focusing on the efficiencies of the best farmers and the newest facilities, . . . the studies present averages largely reflective of the efficiencies of ethanol facilities that are 20 years old.

It often seems that every article, every interview, every public discussion about our most used and visible biofuel, ethanol, starts, and sometimes ends, with the question, "Doesn't it take more energy to make ethanol than is contained in the ethanol?"

In 1980, the short and empirical answer to this question was yes. In 1990, because of improved efficiencies by both farmer and ethanol manufacturer, the answer was, probably not. In 2005 the answer is clearly no.

Yet the question will not go away. One might argue that this is because credible studies by one or two scientists continue to keep alive the claim that biofuels are net energy losers. Yet many grain and oilseed farmers wonder why it is that biofuels like ethanol and biodiesel are singled out for such an aggressive and persistent attack on the net energy issue.

They compare the discussion of biofuels with that of hydrogen, a fuel that has captured the imagination of federal and state governments. Converting the transportation sector (and other sectors as well) to hydrogen has become a national priority. Thousands of articles have been written about hydrogen. Most are wildly enthusiastic. Some are negative. But very, very few even raise the net energy issue.

A Lexis/Nexis search identified over 300 articles published just since 2000 that discuss the energy balance of ethanol, the vast majority with a negative slant; fewer than 5 even mention the net energy issue with respect to hydrogen. Yet for hydrogen the energy balance is not a controversial question. It is well documented that hydrogen's energy balance is negative: It takes more natural gas to make hydrogen from natural gas than is contained in the hydrogen.

Another frustration by biofuels advocates is that the net energy discussion looks backwards, not forwards. Instead of focusing on the efficiencies of the best farmers and the newest facilities and a strategy to make these efficiencies the overall industry and agriculture average, the studies present averages largely reflective of the efficiencies of ethanol facilities that are 20 years old. This is not helpful to long range planning.

Each time a new Pimentel article appears, Cornell University's competent press office broadcasts a provocative press release and news article announcing its latest pessimistic conclusions.

Understanding the Net Energy Debate

The remainder of this paper focuses on the energy balance of biofuels. In doing so, it inevitably focuses largely on the studies of David Pimentel, a Professor of Entomology at Cornell University (now Emeritus). For as long as ethanol has been a matter of public policy, David Pimentel has been its most vocal, sometimes its only, and always its most visible critic.

Pimentel began his association in 1979 when he chaired an advisory committee of the U.S. Department of Energy examining the viability of fuel ethanol (and coal derived methanol).

Since then, Pimentel has authored or co-authored more than 20 technical articles on ethanol. Over time his input and output numbers have varied. But his conclusion remains constant: more fossil fuel energy is needed to grow corn and convert it into ethanol than is contained in the ethanol.

In 2005, still another article by Pimentel appeared. This one was co-authored by Tad Patzek, a professor in the Department of Civil and Environmental Engineering at the University of California, Berkeley. This study raised the net energy debate to a new level by extending the criticism of corn-derived ethanol to ethanol derived from cellulosic materials like wood or switchgrass and to diesel fuel substitutes derived from sunflowers and soybeans. It also insisted, in passing, that ethanol from sugar cane was a net energy loser.

"There is just no energy benefit to using plant biomass for liquid fuel," Pimentel concluded.

Indeed, this latest study reached a remarkable and highly provocative conclusion: the energetics of making ethanol from switchgrass or wood are considerably worse than for making ethanol from corn, and the energetics of making biodiesel from soybeans or sunflowers may be more bleak than making ethanol from corn.

Pimentel's and Patzek's Studies Receive Undeserved Attention

Each time a new Pimentel article appears, Cornell University's competent press office broadcasts a provocative press release and news article announcing its latest pessimistic conclusions, timing its release for maximum visibility. The new article appeared in March 2005 but the press release was issued in July, apparently to coincide with a Congressional vote on an energy bill containing incentives for making ethanol from cellulose and biodiesel from oilseeds.

Each press release invariably leads to a flurry of stories in print and broadcast media throughout the U.S. and Canada and reinvigorates the debate about the efficacy of converting plants into fuels. Each barrage of media coverage elicits detailed rebuttals from the biofuels industries. But these occur after the fact and rarely if ever make it into the mainstream media. Indeed, their very detailed nature inhibits their visibility.

Reporters move on to other stories. After a few weeks the buzz dies down. But the seeds of doubt have been sown and they continue to grow.

Journalists are not to blame for these increasingly predictable cycles of negative publicity regarding biofuels. They lack the time and expertise, even if they have the inclination, to examine competing scientific studies. Those who do undertake such an examination quickly discover how challenging the task can be. For the studies are anything but accessible and transparent. Researchers may use different measures (e.g. high heating values versus low heating values) or different conversion systems (e.g. Btus per gallon versus kilocalories per 1000 liters). Or sometimes even mix measures within a single study (e.g. kilocalories per 1000 liters and kilocalories per 1000 kilograms).

Some studies are very detailed, running to 100 and even 200 pages. Pimentel's studies, on the other hand, are very short, usually consisting of a couple of tables with brief references and brief descriptive text. Pimentel and Patzek's latest study, for example, contains a two paragraph discussion of switchgrass to ethanol, a two paragraph discussion of wood to ethanol, a four paragraph discussion of the energetics of soydiesel and a two paragraph discussion of the energetics of sunflower diesel. All of the text simply repeats numbers from the table. No explanatory discussion is offered.

Few roadmaps are available that highlight the specific areas of disagreement. This commentary attempts to offer such a guide.

Reporters and interested parties who want to examine the numbers and report on or participate in the debate, might take into account six key points.

Pimentel's Conclusion Is Too Broad

1. David Pimentel's pessimism about biofuels derives from a methodological approach that leads him to a far more sweeping and highly controversial conclusion: the world's population has vastly exceeded its biological carrying capacity.

Pimentel's analysis leads him to conclude that the world's population of 6.5 billion people has far surpassed the planet's capacity to feed that population. As he writes, "For the United States to be self-sustaining in solar energy, given our land, water and biological resources, our population should be less than 100 million" . . . (the July 2005 population is 295 million). Pimentel further maintains, "the optimum (world) population should be less than . . . 2 billion."

Pimentel's pessimism about the world's capacity to feed its human population carries over to his view about the limited potential of renewable energy in general. In this he is joined by Patzek, who with Pimentel recently concluded that nuclear power may be the only answer.

> *We want to be very clear: solar cells, wind turbines, and biomass-for-energy plantations can never replace even a small fraction of the highly reliable, 24-hours-a-day, 365-days-a-year, nuclear, fossil, and hydroelectric power stations. Claims to the contrary are popular, but irresponsible . . . new nuclear power stations must be considered.*

Do two-thirds of us have to die in order to allow the remaining third to live a comfortable life on a sustainable basis? Must we rely on nuclear power to provide us a reliable and sufficient source of energy? These questions dwarf that of whether the energy balance of biofuels is slightly negative. One would hope that reporters and others would attend to the catastrophic predictions that result from the full-scale application of Pimentel's methodological approach, rather than the tiny negative impact predicted by its application to a tiny slice of the world's biological resources.

The empirical data overwhelmingly affirm that farmers and ethanol manufacturers are far more energy and resource efficient than they were 20 years ago.

Net Energy Analysis Should Look Forward

2. Policymakers base their decision on whether to aggressively expand biofuels on the latest production technologies and techniques. Therefore, net energy analyses should look forward, not backward. That means, in part, according a higher importance to data from the latest and next-generation manufacturing technologies and agricultural practices over industry averages largely based on the output from older plants.

Averages can be deceiving, particularly in the biofuels industry where until the recent dramatic increase in capacity, the bulk of the industry's manufacturing facilities was 20 years old.

The empirical data overwhelmingly affirm that farmers and ethanol manufacturers are far more energy and resource efficient than they were 20 years ago. The trajectory is positive and the prospects for even further improvement are bright.

Since 1980, for example, new ethanol plants have reduced their energy inputs per gallon of ethanol produced by about 50 percent. In 1980 total energy use was about 69,000 Btus per gallon. Today it is closer to 35,000 Btus. Today, those who invest in ethanol facilities can receive performance guarantees from engineering firms for a thermal efficiency in the low 30,000 Btus per gallon and an electricity efficiency of about 0.76 kWh per gallon.

Pimentel and Patzek's new estimates of the energy balance of making ethanol from cellulose and biodiesel from oil seeds diverge dramatically from those of other studies.

One reason for this reduction in energy inputs is a shift in ethanol production from wet mills to dry mills. Wet mills are more energy intensive than dry mills.

Wet mills were built in the late 1970s and 1980s primarily to manufacture high fructose corn sweetener. They make a variety of products from corn and are more energy intensive than dry mills. They dominated the industry in 1990, producing over 80 percent of all ethanol. In the last 15 years, however, most new ethanol facilities have been dry mills. By 2000 the proportion of production by wet mills had fallen to 55 percent. By the end of 2005 it will be closer to 25 percent. Over 90 percent of all new production now comes from dry mills.

Improved efficiency has come not only in the manufacturing facility but on the farm as well. Since 1980, for example, corn farmers have increased yields from 100 to 140 bushels per acre while using 20–25 percent less fertilizer, herbicide and insecticide per bushel cultivated. A significant number of farmers engage in conservation tillage, a cultivation technique that significantly reduces soil erosion as well as diesel or gasoline use.

Pimentel appears to agree that the trajectory has been positive. He estimates that the amount of energy used to grow a bushel of corn has declined by more than a third between 1991 and 2005 while energy used to make a gallon of ethanol has fallen by about 20 percent.

There Is Greater Disagreement About Cellulosic Ethanol

3. Although an enormous amount of attention has been focused on the debate about the energetics of corn to ethanol, the differences actually have narrowed to the point that they are relatively modest. On the other hand, Pimentel and Patzek's new estimates of the energy balance of making ethanol from cellulose and biodiesel from oil seeds diverge dramatically from those of other studies.

Pimentel's 1991 energetics study of corn derived ethanol found a net energy ratio of 0.68 while his and Patzek's 2005 study estimates a net energy ratio of 0.85. Those who have found a positive ratio estimate it to be in the 1.25–1.4 range. Overall the positive ratios are about 60 percent greater than Pimentel and Patzek's.

On the other hand, Pimentel and Patzek's net energy ratio analysis of biodiesel is 0.98 while those of other studies are in the 2.5–3.2 range, some 150 percent to 200 percent higher.

Pimentel and Patzek cite no studies . . . condemning the energetics of cellulose to ethanol nor biodiesel. We are not aware of any such studies.

Cellulosic ethanol can achieve a positive net energy ratio even higher than that of biodiesel, in large part because the portions of the lignocellulosic [plant biomass that is composed of cellulose, hemicellulose, and lignin] feedstock not converted to ethanol can be burned (or gasified) to provide all of the energy needed for the conversion process.

Thus it would appear more fruitful for the focus to be on the very wide divergence of estimates related to cellulosic ethanol and biodiesel rather than the very modest differences that remain regarding corn derived ethanol.

Pimentel and Patzek Stand Alone

4. All other studies done after 1992, except for Pimentel and Patzek's, have found a positive energy balance of corn to ethanol.

Being in a small minority doesn't mean one is necessarily wrong, but it does indicate the preponderance of scientific opinion is on the other side. Apparently stung by criticism of his loner status, in his latest article Pimentel (and Patzek) insist, "In contrast to the USDA [U.S. Department of Agriculture], numerous scientific studies have concluded that ethanol production does not provide a net energy balance. . . ."

The sources cited in the article do not justify this statement.

Biofuels production overwhelmingly relies on natural gas and coal, not petroleum.

Of the 9 cited, only one was an actual scientific study. That 1989 study found a small 4 percent net energy loss and assumed a very low yield of 90 bushels per acre. Five of the sources were press releases or short statements critical of ethanol that did not analyze net energy issues. The other three contained no independent research. They simply cited Pimentel's data.

Pimentel and Patzek cite no studies, nor press releases or public statements, condemning the energetics of cellulose to ethanol nor biodiesel. We are not aware of any such studies or statements.

Biofuels Reduce Our Dependence on Oil

5. Biofuels displace large quantities of imported oil, regardless of the net energy findings, because their production relies on non-petroleum fuels.

Too often people read about net energy studies that arrive at a negative result and interpret the result this way: "It takes more than a gallon of oil to produce a gallon of ethanol." That is inaccurate. Even Pimentel's studies do not assert this, although he rarely clarifies the distinction between fossils fuels and petroleum.

Biofuels also constitute high quality fuels. They combine energy and storage. . . . This should be taken into account in any comparative energy analysis.

Biofuels production overwhelmingly relies on natural gas and coal, not petroleum. For growing corn and making ethanol from the corn, petroleum (diesel or gasoline) comprises 8–17 percent of the fossil fuel energy used. Coal or natural gas account for the other 83–92 percent (assuming the cellulosic portion of the incoming feedstock is not used to provide thermal and electric energy at the manufacturing plant).

Thus, the net energy ratio with respect to petroleum would be close to 8 to 1. In other words, every Btu of ethanol produced displaces about 8 Btus of petroleum.

For most policymakers, the highest priority of a biofuels policy is to reduce our dependence on imported oil.

Not All Energy Is Created Equal

6. Energy balance analyses should take into account the quality of the energy produced.

The energy content of a fuel is important, but so is the quality of that energy, that is, its usefulness. For example, we use more energy to generate a kilowatt-hour of electricity than is contained in that electricity. But electricity is a high quality fuel, in part because it can be transported easily and in part because it can be used in ways that heat energy cannot. We strive to maximize the amount of electricity we extract from a given amount of heat, but we do not dismiss the utility of electricity because of the energy losses involved in its production.

Biofuels also constitute high quality fuels. They combine energy and storage. Energy from wind and sunlight, on the other hand, is available only intermittently—when the wind blows and the sun shines. Those forms of renewable energy require additional storage systems, like batteries. This should be taken into account in any comparative energy analysis.

Biofuels, like electricity, do require more energy to make than is contained in the fuel. But in the case of biofuels, this additional energy comes from the sun. Solar energy, not fossil fuels, powers the chemical-building photosynthesis process. . . .

A carbohydrate economy . . . is one that can transform the face of agriculture as well as manufacturing, and change the nature of the global agricultural debate.

Three Valuable Studies on Energy Balance

Investigating the energy balance of renewable fuels, indeed, of all fuels, is a worthy endeavor. What puzzles the agricultural community is why biofuels are singled out for such an intense focus on this one issue.

All researchers agree that manufacturers and farmers are becoming more energy and resource efficient, whether in the process of manufacturing equipment or in the raising of crops or producing ethanol. The trajectory is positive and since it is positive, policymakers should focus on what policies could nurture and extend this positive dynamic.

New energy balance studies should focus on the future, not the past. To our knowledge, only three studies have done this. Two were done by my organization, the Institute for Local Self-Reliance. These studies offered, for biodiesel and corn to ethanol, three estimates: current national average energy use in farming and processing; current state best and industry best energy use; next generation manufacturing and state of the art (organic) farming. Michael Graboski's 2002 study also included a section on projected energy use.

While Pimentel and Patzek's estimates of the energy balance of corn to ethanol appear to be converging with other studies, their estimates of the energetics of biodiesel and cellulosic ethanol differ drastically from other studies. Too little information was provided in their report to understand why this is so. But it leads us to recall that the methodology that Pimentel uses, when applied broadly, has led him to conclude that the planet cannot photosynthetically sustain more than a third of the present population. Both Pimentel and Patzek have concluded, based on their methodology, that all renewable resources combined cannot provide sufficient energy to meet our needs. These are very controversial conclusions. It may be more fruitful to examine these methodological conclusions rather than focus on the methodology's application to a tiny slice of the energy and renewable resource sector.

Many of us believe that biological sources can play an important, perhaps even a crucial role in our future economies. They can replace petrochemicals and other products made from fossil fuels. When coupled with a high efficiency transportation system primarily powered by electricity, they can displace petroleum as an engine fuel.

A carbohydrate economy, where plant matter is used as a fuel and industrial material as well as for food and feed and clothing and paper, is one that can transform the face of agriculture as well as manufacturing, and change the nature of the global agricultural debate. But moving in this direction will require a coherent, long term strategy that cuts across sectors and borders. That means tackling fundamental questions, such as the ownership structure of the agricultural industry and world trade negotiations.

We can't tackle these fundamental questions if we continue to spend an inordinate amount of time and intellectual resources poring over net energy studies. Here is one place where one ancient bit of advice seems particularly apt. Let's not lose sight of the forest for the trees.

3

Some Scientists Believe Producing Ethanol from Corn Is Not Energy Efficient

Elizabeth Svoboda

Elizabeth Svoboda is a writer and editor. She has written articles on science and technology for the New York Times, Wired, Popular Science, *and many other publications.*

After having his freshmen class at the University of California, Berkeley, calculate the energy balance of ethanol made from corn, professor Tad Patzek performed an extensive analysis of his own. He concluded that ethanol made from corn contains 65 percent less usable energy than is consumed in its manufacture. In addition, there are other costs to ethanol production, includ- ing damage to the environment caused by fertilizers used to grow the corn itself washing into our rivers and lakes. While Patzek's results are supported by professor David Pimentel of Cornell University, other scientists maintain that Patzek's calculations are based on outdated assumptions about the processes used at each stage of ethanol production.

Ethanol, touted as an alternative fuel of the future, may eat up far more energy during its creation than it winds up giving back, according to research by a UC Berkeley scientist that raises questions about the nation's move toward its wide- spread use.

A clean-burning fuel produced from renewable crops like corn and sugarcane, ethanol has long been a cornerstone of some national lawmakers' efforts to clear the air and curb dependence on foreign oil. California residents use close to a billion gallons of the alcohol-based fuel per year.

Ethanol Takes More Energy to Make than It Provides

But in a recent issue of the journal *Critical Reviews in Plant Sciences*, UC Berkeley geoengineering professor Tad Patzek argued that up to six times more energy is used to make ethanol than the finished fuel actually contains.

Taking grain apart, fermenting it, distilling it and extruding it uses a lot of fossil energy. . . . We are grasping at the solution that is by far the least efficient.

The fossil energy expended during production alone, he concluded, easily outweighs the consumable energy in the end product. As a result, Patzek believes that those who think using the "green" fuel will reduce fossil fuel consumption are deluding themselves—and the federal government's practice of subsidizing ethanol by offering tax exemptions to oil refiners who buy it is a waste of money.

"People tend to think of ethanol and see an endless cycle: corn is used to produce ethanol, ethanol is burned and gives off carbon dioxide, and corn uses the carbon dioxide as it grows," he said. "But that isn't the case. Fossil fuel actually drives the whole cycle."

Patzek's investigation into the energy dynamics of ethanol production began two years ago, when he had the students in his Berkeley freshman seminar calculate the fuel's energy balance as a class exercise.

Once the class took into account little-considered inputs like fossil fuels and other energy sources used to extrude alcohol from corn, produce fertilizers and insecticides, transport crops and dispose of wastewater, they determined that ethanol contains 65 percent less usable energy than is consumed in the process of making it.

Surprised at the results, Patzek began an exhaustive analysis of his own—one that painted an even bleaker picture of the ethanol industry's long-term sustainability.

"Taking grain apart, fermenting it, distilling it and extruding it uses a lot of fossil energy," he said. "We are grasping at the solution that is by far the least efficient."

With hydrogen fuel, people are willing to say, "25 years from now it will be good." Why can't we also be forward-looking when it comes to ethanol?

Other Costs of Ethanol Production

Patzek's report also highlights the potential environmental hazards of ethanol production.

"When you dump nitrogen fertilizer on corn fields, it runs away as surface water, into the Mississippi River and Gulf of Mexico," he said.

The excess nitrogen introduced into the water causes out-of-control algae growth, creating an oxygen-poor "dead zone" where other marine plants and animals cannot survive. And while ethanol produces fewer carbon monoxide emissions than regular gasoline, some researchers have found that ethanol releases high levels of nitrogen oxide, one of the principal ingredients of smog, when burned.

Ethanol has long been touted not just for its promise as a renewable fuel, but for its usefulness as a gasoline additive. Fossil fuels blended with it produce fewer carbon monoxide emissions than regular gasoline and have a higher octane rating, meaning they burn more evenly and are less likely to cause engine knocking. While most gasoline sold in the United States now contains approximately 5 percent ethanol, some cars—such as the Ford Explorer and Chevy Silverado—can run on fuel blends containing up to 85 percent.

Obsolete Data?

Though his work has been vetted by several peer-reviewed scientific journals, Patzek has had to deflect criticism from a variety of sources. David Morris, an economist and vice president of the Minneapolis-based Institute for Local Self-Reliance, has attacked the Berkeley professor's analysis because he says it is based on farming and production practices that are rapidly becoming obsolete.

"His figures (regarding energy consumed in fertilizer production) are accurate for older nitrogen fertilizer plants, but newer plants use only half the energy of those that were built 35 years ago," he said. He also cited the increasing popularity of no-till farming methods, which can reduce a corn farm's diesel usage by 75 percent. "With hydrogen fuel, people are willing to say, '25 years from now it will be good.' Why can't we also be forward-looking when it comes to ethanol?"

Hosein Shapouri, an economist at the U.S. Department of Agriculture, has also cracked down on Patzek's energy calculations.

"It's true that the original ethanol plants in the 1970s went bankrupt. But Patzek doesn't consider the impact new, more efficient production technologies have had on the ethanol industry," he said.

Shapouri's most recent analysis, which the USDA published in 2004, comes to the exact opposite conclusion of Patzek's: Ethanol, he said, has a positive energy balance, containing 67 percent more energy than is used to manufacture it. Optimistic that the process will become even more efficient in the future, he pointed out that scientists are experimenting with using alternative sources like solid waste, grass and wood to make ethanol. If successful on a large scale, these techniques could drastically reduce the amount of fossil fuel needed for ethanol production.

Other contributors to the debate argue that ethanol's net energy balance should not be the sole consideration when policymakers are evaluating its usefulness—factors like the fuel's portability and lower carbon monoxide emissions need to be considered as well.

"So what if we have to spend 2 BTUs for each BTU of alcohol fuel produced?" reads an editorial in the *Offgrid Online* energy newsletter. "Since we are after a portable fuel, we might be willing to spend more energy to get it."

If government funds become short, subsidies for fuels will be looked at very carefully. . . . When they are, there's no way ethanol production can survive.

Are Subsidies Wise?

Cornell University ecology professor David Pimentel, however, sides with Patzek, calling production of ethanol "subsidized food burning."

"The USDA isn't looking at factors like the energy it takes to maintain farm machinery and irrigate fields in their analysis," he said, adding that the agency's ethanol report contains overly optimistic assumptions about the efficiency of farming practices. "The bottom line is that we're using far more energy in making ethanol than we're getting out."

Patzek thinks lawmakers and environmental activists need to push ethanol aside and concentrate on more sustainable solutions like improving the efficiency of fuel cells and hybrid electric cars or harnessing solar energy for use in transport. If they don't, he predicts economics will eventually force the issue.

"If government funds become short, subsidies for fuels will be looked at very carefully," he said. "When they are, there's no way ethanol production can survive."

4

Ethanol Produced from Sources Other than Corn Is Much More Efficient

Deane Morrison

Deane Morrison is a reporter for UMN News *at the University of Minnesota.*

Five University of Minnesota researchers have concluded that ethanol produced from corn provides a modest 25 percent more energy than is consumed in its production. The energy gain from other sources, such as ethanol produced from switchgrass—called cellulosic ethanol—may be much higher. While corn-based ethanol has served a vital role in demonstrating that it is possible to make viable fuels from organic sources, our future energy plan will need to include alternate biofuels. A careful attention to the costs and benefits of each possible fuel source will help to guide wise public policy decisions for the future.

Five University researchers have taken a stand in the long-running debate over whether ethanol from corn requires more fossil fuel energy to produce than it delivers.

Their answer? It delivers 25 percent more energy than is used (mostly fossil fuel) in producing it, though much of that 25 percent energy dividend comes from the production of an ethanol byproduct, animal feed.

Corn Ethanol Is Good, Other Sources Are Better

But the net energy gain is much higher—93 percent—from biodiesel fuel derived from soybeans. And alternative crops such as switchgrass or mixed prairie grasses, which can grow on marginal land with minimal input of fossil fuel derived fertilizers and pesticides, offer the best hope for the future.

Quantifying costs and benefits of biofuels throughout their life cycle allows us to make rational choices and identify better alternatives.

Led by Jason Hill, a postdoctoral associate in the Department of Ecology, Evolution, and Behavior and the Department of Applied Economics, the team published this first comprehensive analysis of the environmental, economic and energetic costs and benefits of ethanol and biodiesel in the pages of the *Proceedings of the National Academy of Sciences.*

"Corn ethanol and soybean biodiesel have proven that we can make viable biofuels," says David Tilman, a coauthor of the study and Regents Professor of Ecology. "This is an important first step toward developing a renewable and environmentally friendly biofuel energy supply, but the challenges ahead are still immense."

A major challenge is getting enough biofuel. Already, 14.3 percent of corn grown in the United States is converted to ethanol, replacing just 1.72 percent of gasoline usage. Even if all the remaining corn were converted to ethanol, the total ethanol would only offset 12 percent of gasoline. The entire soybean crop would replace a much smaller proportion of transportation fuels—only 6 percent of current diesel usage, which itself amounts to a tiny fraction of gasoline usage.

Careful Analysis Leads to Better Policy

With world energy and food demands increasing, the study fills a need for guidance in choosing the best alternative energy strategies. That's why the University's Initiative for Renewable Energy and the Environment (IREE), which aims to make Minnesota a national leader in the development and production of renewable fuels to reduce greenhouse gas emissions and other forms of pollution, helped fund the work.

Biofuels have the potential to provide significant environmental benefits.

"Quantifying costs and benefits of biofuels throughout their life cycle allows us to make rational choices and identify better alternatives," Hill says in a news release.

"The reason for doing this study was to learn from our first two successful biofuels how we could do it better," says Tilman. "It's a bit like the Wright Brothers—a good first start, but if I'm flying across the Atlantic, I want a jet." Besides Hill and Tilman, who is the world's most cited ecologist, study authors were Stephen Polasky and Douglas Tiffany, professors of applied economics; and Erik Nelson, a graduate student in applied economics.

The researchers examined every stage of the biofuels' production and use. They considered such costs as the effort to raise crops, environmental effects of fertilizers and pesticides, transportation and the energy required to distill ethanol.

The analysis showed that growing both corn and soybeans caused soil and water pollution from such chemicals as the nitrogen and phosphorus in fertilizer and from pesticides, with the pesticides used in corn production being especially harmful. But biodiesel used, per unit of energy gained, only 1 percent of the nitrogen, 8.3 percent of the phosphorus and 13 percent of the pesticide (by weight) of corn production.

The researchers also compared greenhouse gas emissions from the two biofuels with emissions caused by producing and burning enough gasoline or diesel to yield the same amount of energy. Emissions from the production and use of corn grain ethanol were 12 percent lower than the net emissions from gasoline; the reduction was 41 percent for biodiesel from soybeans. These figures show that biofuels have the potential to provide significant environmental benefits.

Crops like switchgrass, diverse prairie grasses, and woody plants may offer the best prospects for supplying biofuels.

More Is Better

However, the benefits will only be substantial when much more biofuel is produced and when it has much greater greenhouse gas reductions. For example, if one replaced a total of 5 percent of gasoline energy with ethanol energy, greenhouse gas emissions from driving cars would be a bit more than a half percent lower (5 percent times 12 percent). It must be borne in mind, too, that these figures are only for transportation-related energy usage. Considering total energy use, which includes building heating and electricity, the fraction of savings from transportation biofuels drops by two-thirds.

Also, these reductions hold only for crops grown on land already in production.

"Converting intact ecosystems to production would result in reduced greenhouse gas savings or even net greenhouse gas release from biofuel production," the researchers write.

The researchers noted that rising gasoline and diesel prices have made the development of biofuels more economically advantageous, and that biodiesel's environmental benefits seem strong enough to merit subsidy. Yet ethanol also plays an important role as an additive by oxygenating gasoline and making it burn more cleanly.

"New and better transportation biofuels and greatly increased energy efficiency are essential for our economy and our environment," says Tilman. "We also need renewable electricity, including both wind energy and renewable biofuels that take the place of coal. Coal is a major source of electricity and of greenhouse gases."

The researchers point to nonfood plants that can grow on marginal lands with minimal input of fertilizers and pesticides as the best hope for bio-based energy. Crops like switchgrass, diverse prairie grasses, and woody plants may offer the best prospects for supplying biofuels. Researchers at the University and elsewhere are hard at work finding ways to tap the energy of such plants, which is locked up in difficult-to-digest cellulose and related plant materials. One thing that made corn and soybeans so attractive in the first place was the relative ease of extracting energy from the carbohydrates and oils in those crops. But with global warming rapidly changing the world environment, and energy prices soaring, there is no choice but to find alternative sources of energy, and fast.

5

Corn-Based Ethanol Drives up the Retail Price of Food

Economist

The Economist *is a weekly magazine covering current events, politics, and financial news through the lens of free market economic theory.*

There has been a substantial increase in world food prices recently, which surprisingly has occurred during a period of great abundance. While this is partly due to increased consumption of meat, especially in India and China, the primary cause is the increased use of corn for the production of ethanol in the United States. If current trends continue, there will be winners and losers. While farmers throughout the world will benefit, it is primarily the poor who will suffer. Governments can act to alleviate the suffering, but some potential solutions—subsidizing the income of the poor, for example—will work much better than others, such as continued subsidization of corn production or caps on the price of food.

One of the odder features of last weekend's [early December 2007] vote in Venezuela was that staple foods were in short supply. Something similar happened in Russia before its parliamentary election. Governments in both oil-rich countries had imposed controls on food prices, with the usual consequences. Such controls have been surprisingly widespread—a knee-jerk response to one of the most remarkable changes that food markets, indeed any markets, have seen for years: the end of cheap food.

In early September [2007] the world price of wheat rose to over $400 a tonne, the highest ever recorded. In May it had been around $200. Though in real terms its price is far below the heights it scaled in 1974, it is still twice the average of the past 25 years. Earlier this year the price of maize (corn) exceeded $175 a tonne, again a world record. It has fallen from its peak, as has that of wheat, but at $150 a tonne is still 50% above the average for 2006.

What is most remarkable about the present bout of "agflation" is that record prices are being achieved at a time not of scarcity but of abundance.

As the price of one crop shoots up, farmers plant it to take advantage, switching land from other uses. So a rise in wheat prices has knock-on effects on other crops. Rice prices have hit records this year, although their rise has been slower. *The Economist*'s food-price index is now at its highest since it began in 1845, having risen by one-third in the past year [2007].

Rising Food Prices in an Era of Abundance

Normally, sky-high food prices reflect scarcity caused by crop failure. Stocks are run down as everyone lives off last year's stores. This year [2007] harvests have been poor in some places, notably Australia, where the drought-hit wheat crop failed for the second year running. And world cereals stocks as a proportion of production are the lowest ever recorded. The run-down has been accentuated by the decision of large countries (America and China) to reduce stocks to save money.

Yet what is most remarkable about the present bout of "agflation" is that record prices are being achieved at a time not of scarcity but of abundance. According to the International Grains Council, a trade body based in London, this year's total cereals crop will be 1.66 billion tonnes, the largest on record and 89m tonnes more than last year's harvest, another bumper crop. That the biggest grain harvest the world has ever seen is not enough to forestall scarcity prices tells you that something fundamental is affecting the world's demand for cereals.

America is easily the world's largest maize exporter—and it now uses more of its maize crop for ethanol than it sells abroad.

The Meat of the Question

Two things, in fact. One is increasing wealth in China and India. This is stoking demand for meat in those countries, in turn boosting the demand for cereals to feed to animals. The use of grains for bread, tortillas and *chapattis* is linked to the growth of the world's population. It has been flat for decades, reflecting the slowing of population growth. But demand for meat is tied to economic growth and global GDP is now in its fifth successive year of expansion at a rate of 4%-plus.

Higher incomes in India and China have made hundreds of millions of people rich enough to afford meat and other foods. In 1985 the average Chinese consumer ate 20kg (44lb) of meat a year; now he eats more than 50kg. China's appetite for meat may be nearing satiation, but other countries are following behind: in developing countries as a whole, consumption of cereals has been flat since 1980, but demand for meat has doubled.

Not surprisingly, farmers are switching, too: they now feed about 200m–250m more tonnes of grain to their animals than they did 20 years ago. That increase alone accounts for a significant share of the world's total cereals crop. Calorie for calorie, you need more grain if you eat it transformed into meat than if you eat it as bread: it takes three kilograms of cereals to produce a kilo of pork, eight for a kilo of beef. So a shift in diet is multiplied many times over in the grain markets. Since the late 1980s an inexorable annual increase of 1–2% in the demand for feedgrains has ratcheted up the overall demand for cereals and pushed up prices.

According to the World Bank, the grain needed to fill up an SUV would feed a person for a year.

Rising Demand for Ethanol

Because this change in diet has been slow and incremental, it cannot explain the dramatic price movements of the past year. The second change can: the rampant demand for ethanol as fuel for American cars. In 2000 around 15m tonnes of America's maize crop was turned into ethanol; this year [2007] the quantity is likely to be around 85m tonnes. America is easily the world's largest maize exporter—and it now uses more of its maize crop for ethanol than it sells abroad.

Ethanol is the dominant reason for this year's [2007] increase in grain prices. It accounts for the rise in the price of maize because the federal government has in practice waded into the market to mop up about one-third of America's corn harvest. A big expansion of the ethanol programme in 2005 explains why maize prices started rising in the first place.

Ethanol accounts for some of the rise in the prices of other crops and foods too. Partly this is because maize is fed to animals, which are now more expensive to rear. Partly it is because America's farmers, eager to take advantage of the biofuels bonanza, went all out to produce maize this year [2007], planting it on land previously devoted to wheat and soyabeans. This year [2007] America's maize harvest will be a jaw-dropping 335m tonnes, beating last year's by more than a quarter. The increase has been achieved partly at the expense of other food crops.

This year [2007] the overall decline in stockpiles of all cereals will be about 53m tonnes—a very rough indication of by how much demand is outstripping supply. The increase in the amount of American maize going just to ethanol is about 30m tonnes. In other words, the demands of America's ethanol programme alone account for over half the world's unmet need for cereals. Without that programme, food prices would not be rising anything like as quickly as they have been. According to the World Bank, the grain needed to fill up an SUV would feed a person for a year.

The Effect of Subsidies

America's ethanol programme is a product of government subsidies. There are more than 200 different kinds, as well as a 54 cents-a-gallon tariff on imported ethanol. That keeps out greener Brazilian ethanol, which is made from sugar rather than maize. Federal subsidies alone cost $7 billion a year (equal to around $1.90 a gallon).

Because supplies will not match increases in demand, . . .
cereal prices will rise by between 10% and 20% by 2015.

In theory, what governments mandate, they can also scrap. But that seems unlikely with oil at the sort of price that makes them especially eager to promote alternative fuels. Subsidies might be trimmed, of course, reducing demand occasionally; this is happening a bit now. And eventually, new technologies to convert biomass to liquid fuel will replace ethanol—but that will take time. For the moment, support for the ethanol programme seems secure. Hillary Clinton and John McCain used to be against ethanol subsidies, but have changed their minds. Russia and Venezuela are not the only countries that like to meddle in food markets for political reasons.

So demand for grain will probably remain high for a while. Demand, though, is only one side of the equation. Supply forms the other. If there is a run of bumper harvests, prices will fall back; if not, they will stay high.

Harvests can rise only if new land is brought into cultivation or yields go up. This can happen fairly quickly. The world's cereal farmers responded enthusiastically to price signals by planting more high-value crops. And so messed-up is much of the rich world's farming systems that farmers in the West have often been paid not to grow crops—something that can easily be reversed, as happened this year when the European Union suspended the "set aside" part of its common agricultural policy. Still, there are limits to how much harvests can be expanded in the short term. In general, says a new report by the International Food Policy Research Institute (IFPRI), which is financed by governments and development banks, the response tends to be sticky: a 10% rise in prices yields a 1–2% increase in supply.

In the longer run, plenty of new farmland could be ploughed up and many technological gains could be had. But much of the new land is in remote parts of Brazil, Russia, Kazakhstan, the Congo and Sudan: it would require big investments in roads and other infrastructure, which could take decades—and would often lead to the clearing of precious forest. Big gains could be had if genetically modified foods were brought into production or if new seed varieties were planted in Africa. But again, that will take time. Moreover, GM foods will not live up to their promise unless they shed the popular suspicion that dogs them, especially in Europe. And some of the new land—dry, marginal areas of Africa, Brazil and Kazakhstan—could be vulnerable to damage from global warming. By some measures, global warming could cut world farm output by as much as one-sixth by 2020. No less worryingly, high oil prices would depress the use of oil-based fertilisers, which have been behind much of the increase in farm production during the past half-century.

High Prices Are Likely Here to Stay

It is risky to predict long-run trends in farming—technology in particular always turns out unexpectedly—but most forecasters conclude from these conflicting currents that prices will stay high for as much as a decade. Because supplies will not match increases in demand, IFPRI believes, cereal prices will rise by between 10% and 20% by 2015. The UN's Food and Agriculture Organisation's forecast for 2016–17 is slightly higher. Whatever the exact amount, this year's agflation seems unlikely to be, as past rises have been, simply the upward side of a spike.

If prices do not fall back, this will mark a break with the past. For decades, prices of cereals and other foods have been in decline, both in the shops and on world markets. The IMF's index of food prices in 2005 was slightly lower than it had been in 1974, which means that in real terms food prices fell during those 30 years by three-quarters. In the 1960s food (including meals out) accounted for one-quarter of the average American's spending; by 2005 the share was less than one-seventh.

In other words, were food prices to stay more or less where they are today, it would be a radical departure from a past in which shoppers and farmers got used to a gentle decline in food prices year in, year out. It would put an end to the era of cheap food. And its effects would be felt everywhere, but especially in countries where food matters most: poor ones.

Developing countries as a whole will spend over $50 billion importing cereals this year [2007], 10% more than last.

A Blessing and a Curse

If you took your cue from governments, you would conclude that dearer food was unequivocally a bad thing. About a score of countries have imposed food-price controls of some sort. Argentina, Morocco, Egypt, Mexico and China have put restraints on domestic prices. A dozen countries, including India, Vietnam, Serbia and Ukraine, have imposed export taxes or limited exports. Argentina and Russia have done both. In all these places governments are seeking to shelter their people from food-price rises by price controls. But dearer food is not a pure curse: it produces winners as well as losers.

Obviously, farmers benefit—if governments allow them to keep the gains. In America, the world's biggest agricultural exporter, net farm income this year will be $87 billion, 50% more than the average of the past ten years. The prairie farmers of the Midwest are looking forward to their Caribbean cruises.

Other beneficiaries are in poor countries. Food exporters such as India, South Africa and Swaziland will gain from increased export earnings. Countries such as Malawi and Zimbabwe, which used to export food but no longer do so, also stand to gain if they can boost their harvests. Given that commodity prices have been falling for so long in real terms, this would be an enormous relief to places that have suffered from a relentless decline in their terms of trade.

In emerging markets an income gap has opened up between cities and countryside over the past few years. As countries have diversified away from agriculture into industry and services, urban wages have outstripped rural ones. Income inequality is conventionally measured using a scale running from zero to one called the Gini coefficient. A score of 0.5 is the mark of a highly unequal society. The Asian Development Bank reckons that China's Gini coefficient rose from 0.41 in 1993 to 0.47 in 2004. If farm incomes in poor countries are pushed up by higher food prices, that could mitigate the growing gap between city and countryside. But will it?

Guess Who Loses

According to the World Bank, 3 billion people live in rural areas in developing countries, of whom 2.5 billion are involved in farming. That 3 billion includes three-quarters of the world's poorest people. So in principle the poor overall should gain from higher farm incomes. In practice many will not. There are large numbers of people who lose more from higher food bills than they gain from higher farm incomes. Exactly how many varies widely from place to place.

In general, it is better to subsidise poor peoples' incomes, rather than food prices.

Among the losers from higher food prices are big importers. Japan, Mexico and Saudi Arabia will have to spend more to buy their food. Perhaps they can afford it. More worryingly, some of the poorest places in Asia (Bangladesh and Nepal) and Africa (Benin and Niger) also face higher food bills. Developing countries as a whole will spend over $50 billion importing cereals this year [2007], 10% more than last.

Rising prices will also hurt the most vulnerable of all. The World Food Programme, the main provider of emergency food aid, says the cost of its operations has increased by more than half in the past five years [2003–2007] and will rise by another third in the next two [2008–2009]. Food-aid flows have fallen to their lowest level since 1973.

In every country, the least well-off consumers are hardest hit when food prices rise. This is true in rich and poor countries alike but the scale in the latter is altogether different. As Gary Becker, a Nobel economics laureate at the University of Chicago, points out, if food prices rise by one-third, they will reduce living standards in rich countries by about 3%, but in very poor ones by over 20%.

Not all consumers in poor countries are equally vulnerable. The food of the poor in the Andes, for example, is potatoes; in Ethiopia, teff: neither is traded much across borders, so producers and consumers are less affected by rising world prices. As the World Bank's annual *World Development Report* shows, the number of urban consumers varies from over half the total number of poor in Bolivia, to about a quarter in Zambia and Ethiopia, to less than a tenth in Vietnam and Cambodia.

[Agflation] is likely to help shift the balance of power in the world economy further towards emerging markets.

But overall, enormous numbers of the poor—both urban and landless labourers—are net buyers of food, not net sellers. They have already been hard hit: witness the riots that took place in Mexico over tortilla prices earlier this year [2007]. According to IFPRI, the expansion of ethanol and other biofuels could reduce calorie intake by another 4–8% in Africa and 2–5% in Asia by 2020. For some countries, such as Afghanistan and Nigeria, which are only just above subsistence levels, such a fall in living standards could be catastrophic.

Some Solutions Are Better than Others

So it is no good saying "let them eat cake": there are strong welfare arguments for helping those who stand to lose. But the way you do it matters. In general, it is better to subsidise poor peoples' incomes, rather than food prices: this distorts price signals the least and allows farmers to benefit from higher prices. Where it is not possible to subsidise incomes (because to do so requires a decent civil service), it is still possible to minimise the unintended consequences if food subsidies are targeted and temporary. Morocco fixed bread prices (the food of the poor) during Ramadan, the Muslim month of fasting; at the same time, it cut tariffs on food imports to increase competition.

In contrast, Russia shows how not to do it. It imposed across-the-board price controls on milk, eggs, bread and other staples, benefiting everyone whether they needed help or not. Food is disappearing from shelves and farmers are bearing the brunt. As Don Mitchell of the World Bank points out, "if you want to help consumers, you can do it without destroying your producers but only if you go about it in the right way." In reality, many of the recent price controls are blatant politicking. About half the countries that imposed price controls did so before elections or other big political events. Russia's are due to run out just after next year's presidential election. Funny, that.

Emerging Economies May Benefit

There is one last important knock-on effect of agflation. It is likely to help shift the balance of power in the world economy further towards emerging markets. Higher food prices have increased inflation around the world, but by different amounts in different countries. In Europe and America food accounts for only about one-tenth of the consumer-price index, so even though food prices in rich countries rising by around 5% a year, it has not made a big difference. There have been clucks of concern from the European Central Bank and a consumer boycott of pasta in Italy, but that is about all.

In poor countries, in contrast, food accounts for half or more of the consumer-price index (over two-thirds in Bangladesh and Nigeria). Here, higher food prices have had a much bigger impact. Inflation in food prices in emerging markets nearly doubled in the past year [2007], to 11%; meat and egg prices in China have gone up by almost 50% (although that is partly because pork prices have been pushed up by a disease in pigs). This has dragged up headline inflation in emerging markets from around 6% in 2006 to over 8% now. In many countries, inflation is at its highest for a decade.

Central bankers are determined to ensure that what could be a one-off shift in food prices does not create continuing inflation by pushing up wages or creating expectations of higher prices. So they are tightening monetary policy. China increased interest rates in August [2007], Chile in July [2007], Mexico in May [2007]. The striking thing about these rises is that they are the opposite of what has been happening in some rich countries. The Federal Reserve reduced rates by 50 basis points in September [2007] and 25 points in October [2007]; the Bank of Canada cut rates this week [early December, 2007]. The indirect effect of food-price rises has therefore been to widen the interest-rate differential between rich and emerging markets.

And all this is going on as the economic balance of power is shifting. Growth in America and Europe is slowing; China and India are going great guns. Financial confidence in the West has been shaken by the subprime-mortgage crisis; capital flows into emerging markets are setting records.

This shift will be tricky to handle. Such transitions always are. The risk is of a bubble in emerging markets. As Simon Johnson, the IMF'S director of research, wryly notes, "every bubble starts with a change in the real economy." Food markets are an obvious place to start. How emerging countries fare—and how poor consumers cope—depends on their economic policies. The imposition of food-price controls was not exactly a good start.

6

Corn-Based Ethanol Does Not Significantly Affect the Retail Price of Food

Ethanol Across America

Ethanol Across America is a nonprofit, nonpartisan education campaign of the Clean Fuels Foundation and is sponsored by industry, government, and private interests. This essay is part of a continuing series and was sponsored by the American Coalition for Ethanol, the Clean Fuels Development Coalition, the Maryland Grain Producers Utilization Board, the Nebraska Ethanol Board, and the Nebraska Public Power District.

Critics of ethanol claim that, as a society, we must choose between using our agricultural resources for feeding people or for fueling cars. Although corn prices in America have risen in response to increased demand for ethanol—in part due to governmental support such as the renewable fuel standard in the Energy Policy Act of 2005—we can continue to meet both goals. Because most of the retail price of food reflects processing costs and other added value, rather than the cost of raw materials, an increase in corn prices has little effect on the price American consumers pay for food. Furthermore, the productivity and efficiency of America's corn farmers has steadily risen over the past three decades, and this trend can be expected to continue in the future. Combined with greater efficiency in the production of ethanol, this means that American farmers will be able to increase the supply of corn to make up for the expected rise in demand.

Ethanol Across America, "Issue Brief: The Impact of Ethanol Production on Food, Feed, and Fuel," Summer 2007. Reproduced by permission. http://www.ethanol.org/pdf/contentmgmt/Issue_Brief_food_feed_fuel.pdf.

For more than three decades, critics have tried to cast ethanol as a "food versus fuel" argument. The marketplace is a better indicator of grain supply and demands—and statistics simply don't bear out the dire predictions of those who say we must choose between fueling our cars and feeding people. We can do both—and we are.

The process of producing ethanol and high-protein co-products from grain has been practiced for centuries. Using ethanol as a fuel was first advocated more than 100 years ago. The first extensive use of ethanol in gasoline was adopted as part of a domestic energy strategy in the 1970s. Ethanol was used as an octane replacement in the 1980s and as a tool in the battle against air pollution in the 1990s. Today, ethanol meets a host of energy, agricultural, rural development and economic policy objectives.

Legitimate concerns about the impact of increased demand for corn and other grains can be addressed without inciting emotional and distorted rhetoric.

Increased Demand for Ethanol

The increasing demand for cleaner transportation fuels creates great opportunities for biofuels—agriculture-derived renewable fuels such as ethanol and biodiesel. Production of ethanol in the United States reached an historic high level in 2006—a trend that is expected to continue. While sorghum, sugar crops and waste materials are used to produce ethanol, corn will continue to be the primary source of U.S.-produced ethanol for at least another decade.

The implementation of a national Renewable Fuels Standard (RFS) is a key factor in expansion of ethanol use nationally. The removal of MTBE [a gasoline additive] as an oxygenate, the use of ethanol as an octane enhancer and continued public policy initiatives focused on renewable energy continue to drive demand for ethanol and other biofuels.

After years of cheap corn, American farmers are finally seeing the fruits of their investment in the development of the ethanol industry as corn prices have surged of late. How would you like to work for 25 years and not get a raise? That's what American corn farmers have experienced until now.

While the increase in corn prices pales in comparison to that of energy costs, there are concerns about the effect of corn demand on food supplies and food prices.

As the ethanol industry grows, increased demand for corn will create challenges and opportunities for consumers, livestock producers, policy makers and refiners. Legitimate concerns about the impact of increased demand for corn and other grains can be addressed without inciting emotional and distorted rhetoric.

Food and Fuel, not Food vs. Fuel

The conversion of grain to ethanol and other co-products is relatively simple. The starch and fiber are converted to ethanol and a variety of other products, depending on the process used.

A "dry mill" process is the most common technology and is used in about 80% of U.S. ethanol plants. This is a basic but technologically innovative process that converts a bushel of corn into three products that differ in volume, but are nearly equal in weight.

Basically, one bushel of corn yields one-third its weight in ethanol, one-third in high protein livestock feed (called "distillers grains") and one-third in carbon dioxide, which can be used for food and beverage processing and industrial applications.

"Wet mill" plants are basically corn refineries that convert various components of the corn kernel into food, feed, fuel and industrial products. Representing about 20% of ethanol plants in the U.S., these wet mill facilities tend to be larger and more expensive than dry mill plants due to the complexity and diversity of products.

Less than 12% of the nation's field corn crop is processed directly into human food products in the United States.

How Much Corn Is in a Box of Corn Flakes?

Ethanol critics have focused attention on the effect that increased corn use may have on food prices. It's a legitimate issue, but must be put in context.

The raw material in many products is a very small portion of the cost paid by the consumer—and this is especially true in food processing. This is particularly the case in food products using grain, in which an abundant supply is converted into value-added products such as cereal, bread or meat.

Farmers and livestock producers seldom own the processing factory and typically have little to do with packaging and marketing the product. Costs for these functions are added as the product moves to market. For example, 68% of the retail price of beef and pork goes to the "middle men" involved in the food processing and distribution chain.

Ethanol critics routinely overstate how much corn is actually consumed as human food. Less than 12% of the nation's field corn crop is processed directly into human food products in the United States. Corn syrup, sweeteners, starches and cereals are examples. Corn demand for the human food market has been flat over recent years. The majority of field corn is fed to livestock, exported or processed into ethanol and its co-products.

The Truth About Food Prices

Despite extensive media coverage about the potential for a significant increase in food prices due to corn demand for ethanol, statistics simply do not support this claim.

The *Chicago Tribune* claimed that using corn for ethanol would raise the price of corn to such an extent that consumer meat prices would rise drastically, adding "the conversion of corn into ethanol would destroy our meat industry."

That was in 1995.

More than 10 years later, U.S. consumers continue to enjoy the most affordable and abundant food supply in the world—in spite of a surge in corn demand for ethanol production.

There is no question that corn prices have risen dramatically in recent months, but the effect on consumer prices has, by all accounts, been negligible—or non-existent. The U.S. Commerce Department Consumer Price Index (CPI) released in April 2007 shows that from January 2006 to March 2007, a timeframe when corn prices nearly doubled, consumer food costs increased by less than average: 2.1% compared to the 25-year average of 2.9%. According to the National Corn Growers Association, history shows that farm-gate corn prices and retail meat prices are unrelated.

An increase in corn prices will have a nominal effect on total household spending. But consider how the cost of gasoline impacts consumer costs. When crude oil moved from $40 per barrel to $70 per barrel, consumers faced a 75% increase in fuel prices. That hits the pocketbook hard—making it more expensive to get to the grocery store in the first place.

Higher energy prices drive food prices up—affecting not only raw material production (grain, etc.), but the cost of processing and transporting products to the marketplace.

There are some who say that years of cheap corn have actually fueled consolidation in the food processing industry, which can in turn lead to a less-competitive marketplace. According to syndicated [agriculture] columnist Alan Guebert: "The flood of institutionalized, cheap feed lifted the biggest boats the highest. . . . The cheap feed caused a chain reaction: huge profits funded the continued integration of the meat industry."

More Ethanol Production Means More Livestock Feed

The important role of a co-product of ethanol production is often overlooked by ethanol critics. About one third of each corn kernel is converted to distillers grains—a high-protein feed for livestock. As the production of ethanol increases, so does the supply of this valuable feed source.

Farmers planted 92.9 million acres of corn [in 2007]—an increase of 14.5 million acres over the previous year.... This increase will easily absorb the demand from new ethanol plants.

Livestock nutritionists have documented that, when fed as part of a balanced ration, distillers grains often outperform a corn-dominated diet. Distillers grains have become an important nutritional resource for livestock producers, especially in beef and dairy production.

Distillers grains displace a portion of the corn used in swine and poultry rations. Research and technology innovations are underway to increase distillers grains' value for these species.

The displacement of corn with distillers grains allows corn to be used for other purposes. Additionally, improvements in processing and application of corn and other grains used in ethanol production will serve as a hedge against higher food prices.

Meeting the Demand for More Corn

The corn supply is not static—and ethanol is just one factor in the corn demand equation.

America's farmers are the most efficient and productive in the world. In 2006, U.S. corn farmers produced a near record 10.74 billion bushels of corn. Of that, 1.8 billion bushels went to the production of ethanol and co-products. (It's important to note that ethanol production also consumed about 26 percent of the nation's grain sorghum crop in 2006.)

In 2007, farmers responded to market signals (as they always have) and geared up to fulfill the demand for more corn. In June 2007, the USDA [U.S. Department of Agriculture] National Agricultural Statistics Service reported that farmers planted 92.9 million acres of corn—an increase of 14.5 million acres over the previous year. Much of this came from the conversion of cotton and soybean acres to corn.

This increase will easily absorb the demand from new ethanol plants coming on line in 2008 and beyond, with more than one billion new bushels available.

The ongoing innovation in crop genetics and technology continues to help farmers produce more bushels on the same acres. Based on recent estimates, U.S. corn farmers have the potential to produce 15 billion to 16 billion bushels annually by 2015—perhaps as much as 18 billion bushels. Of this crop, one-third could be used in ethanol production—providing enough corn for 15 billion to 20 billion gallons of ethanol. That would leave a minimum of 12 billion bushels for feed, food and export markets—up from 9.5 billion bushels in 2006.

How is this possible? Because agronomic productivity (corn yield per acre) and process efficiency (ethanol yield per bushel) continue to improve. The potential for increased corn-to-ethanol production is based on a progression of commercial results that have already been demonstrated and thus have a high degree of certainty.

Better Technology Will Increase Supply

Agronomic productivity reflects the combination of optimized planting rates, nutrient management and biotechnology that has helped producers reduce the impact of insects, disease and pressure from competitive vegetation. This leads to increased yield and reduced variability in yields from year to year.

Since 1961, yields have increased 1.8% annually—indicating that yields of 180 bushels per acre are possible by 2015. Even more telling, yield increases since 2001 have averaged 2.8% annually, thanks in large part to the broad adoption of transgenic hybrids. Using these trends, a 200 bushel per acre average is possible by 2015.

A number of advancements in corn and ethanol production are leading to greater efficiency—squeezing more ethanol out of each kernel.

It would be false to assume these dramatic yield increases are the result of over-fertilization. According to the ProExporter Network, the yield per acre increased 27 percent from 1988 to 2004; yet the average application of nitrogen fertilizer increased just 10 percent during the same period.

Even some of ethanol's most vocal critics on the use of corn concede this important point about the constant increases in yield. In a 2007 study funded in part by the American Meat Institute, National Cattlemen's Beef Association, National Pork Producers Council and several other groups with an interest in seeing grain prices remain low, one of the scenarios for ethanol growth was determined to have little impact on grain price increases.

The study projects that even if ethanol production experiences a 150% increase over current levels, "yield gains ultimately would provide sufficient additional corn stocks to moderate grain price increases. . . ."

The dire predictions of ethanol opponents and others only surface when the usage scenarios go beyond current ethanol projections and often incorporate extremes such as droughts, low oil prices and other factors that support their claims.

Studies based on rational assumptions conclude that ethanol production would have little impact on grain prices under projected growth levels.

Lastly, the study predicts corn prices will level off at $3.16 per bushel—an amount unlikely to appreciably impact grain or food prices.

Making More Ethanol from the Same Kernel of Corn

Corn will continue to be the domestic feedstock of choice for ethanol production in the near term. A number of advancements in corn and ethanol production are leading to greater efficiency—squeezing more ethanol out of each kernel.

Ethanol yield has already improved from 2.4 gallons per bushel in the 1980s to 2.8 gallons in modern plants. Corn hybrids developed specifically for ethanol production have demonstrated ethanol yield increases of 2.7 percent—and using the cellulose (fiber) in the corn kernel (in addition to the starch) could increase yield by 10 to 13 percent. Enzymes are already available that assist in the breakdown and conversion of corn kernel cellulose.

[The] geographic expansion of ethanol production will serve to strengthen America's economy and energy security without jeopardizing our abundant food supplies.

With this combination of hybrid and plant process optimization, theoretical yields of 3.51 gallons of ethanol per bushel are within reason—with no negative impact on protein or oil content for animal feed uses of the co-product.

Other Crops Will Add to Ethanol Production

Corn and other grains will remain the primary source of U.S. ethanol production during the next decade. However, American farmers will eventually become vital suppliers of cellulosic material for ethanol production as well.

Biomass materials such as corn stalks, wheat straw, switchgrass and other renewable feedstocks will contribute to the resource base available for energy use. It is estimated that America can supply a sustainable volume of biomass materials in excess of 1.3 billion tons per year—enough to produce approximately 60 billion gallons of ethanol each year.

As cellulose-to-ethanol technologies build on grain-to-ethanol capabilities, America will remain a world leader in ethanol production. From forestry wastes to agriculture residues, from municipal waste to new energy crops, technology innovations will transform renewable resources into ethanol across the nation and around the world.

This geographic expansion of ethanol production will serve to strengthen America's economy and energy security without jeopardizing our abundant food supplies. The ethanol industry will continue to be a strategic supplier of both food and fuel for the future.

7

Ethanol Is Popular with Politicians, But Experts Have Concerns

Marianne Lavelle and Bret Schulte

Marianne Lavelle is a senior writer on energy policy and utilities for U.S. News & World Report. She is also coauthor of the book Toxic Deception: How the Chemical Industry Manipulates Science, Bends the Law, and Endangers Your Health. *Bret Schulte is a contributing writer for* U.S. News & World Report.

Ethanol's promise of reducing America's dependence on foreign oil while simultaneously revitalizing the economy of many rural communities has been impossible for politicians to resist. It has become difficult to find anyone in Washington who is not at least guardedly optimistic about ethanol, especially during a presidential election cycle. Scientists and economists, however, point out that there are many questions about ethanol that have not been answered yet. Potential problems include ethanol's environmental impact, the effect of increased ethanol production on the price of food, and the practical limitations of currently existing ethanol technologies and infrastructure.

[G]alva, Iowa—a] farming town of fewer than 400 people—might be most memorable for what it doesn't have: a Wal-Mart, a high school, even a stoplight. But humble Galva and its environs have two things in abundance: corn and, by extension, hope.

Marianne Lavelle and Bret Schulte, "Is Ethanol the Answer?" *U.S. News & World Report*, February 4, 2007. Reprinted with permission. http://www.usnews.com.

"We feel we're on the cusp here as far as things happening," says Rita Frahm, an 18-year resident and president of the county's economic development corporation. That's because Galva is the lucky home of an ethanol plant.

There's a lot of exaggeration about what ethanol is capable of doing.

Since opening in 2002, the plant has produced ever increasing dividends, to date putting more than $13 million into the hands of the 420 local farmers and investors who own it. That cash is slowly but markedly changing Galva's landscape. For the first time in 30 years, the town witnessed construction of three new homes at once, and a whole new street, Sixth Street, on which to place the houses. Those dwellings are now occupied by families "who saw an opportunity to stay rather than the community dying," Frahm says.

Heartwarming stories like Galva's—in a state that hosts the first presidential contest—help explain why Washington is so fired up over ethanol. In 2006, production skyrocketed, and Washington is poised to push it still higher. What's not to like? Every gallon theoretically means more money for the iconic American farmer and less cash lining the pockets of foreign sheiks. "There's almost a sense," says Iowa State University political scientist Steffen Schmidt, "that ethanol is morally better than oil."

Washington loves a "win-win," but there are plenty of doubts as to whether the love affair with ethanol qualifies. Even though the ethanol industry profited handsomely last year, it continued to benefit from billions of dollars in taxpayer subsidies. And as ethanol becomes a larger part of the energy mix, it is not clear that Washington is prepared for the fallout. Ethanol already consumes so much corn that signs of strain on the food supply and prices are rippling across the marketplace. Environmental impacts will multiply as more land and water are devoted to the prized yellow grain. And, even if these problems were overcome, ethanol's potential growth could be stunted by an energy system currently tailored to gasoline. Ethanol undoubtedly plays a role in the quest for energy independence and the desire to curb global warming. But some observers worry that ethanol development may take the place of more effective initiatives: forcing automakers to increase gas mileage, for instance, or mandating cuts in carbon dioxide emissions. "Some members of Congress are looking for quick fixes," says one economist who has studied the issue. "It's an easy bandwagon to jump on. But there's a lot of exaggeration about what ethanol is capable of doing."

The 10 largest ethanol producers and their trade groups have handed out $4.7 million in federal campaign contributions [between 2000 and early 2007].

The Rise of Ethanol

Ethanol is alcohol distilled from fermented, mashed grain. It took a century for it to make a big splash on the U.S. energy scene, even though Henry Ford built his first Model T in 1908 to run on either gasoline or ethanol. Over the decades, petroleum proved cheaper, and grain alcohol was relegated to college fraternity parties rather than gas tanks. No one looked seriously at ethanol as fuel until the oil price shocks of the 1970s, when Congress decided to subsidize a homegrown alternative—most significantly through a tax credit to oil companies for every gallon of the costly alternative they blended into gasoline. But when oil prices fell again in the late 1980s through the 1990s, the nation's dependence on petroleum imports mushroomed to 60 percent, and ethanol was reduced to a performance-boosting additive for some midwestern gasoline—a nice, subsidized side business for the dominant producer, Archer Daniels Midland.

Around 2000, ethanol started gaining traction when it emerged as the substitute to methyl tertiary butyl ether (MTBE), an oxygenate that reduced air pollution but leaked into drinking water at potentially dangerous levels. At the same time, upstart businesses like VeraSun of Brookings, S.D., were learning to produce ethanol more efficiently. Then came the Iraq war and high oil prices. Suddenly, the price ethanol refiners could fetch for their product from the big oil companies was far higher than the production cost. In places like Galva, where farmers had pooled their money to put up plants earlier, returns rolled in. It was a modern-day gold rush for grain farmers and investors. Today, 60 percent of ethanol production is in the hands of small companies.

Ethanol Enters the Political Arena

The rush of new players strengthened the industry's clout. One of the largest stakes in the No. 2 producer, VeraSun, for instance, is owned by a midwestern venture capital firm, Bluestem, founded by Steve Kirby, former lieutenant governor of South Dakota and a big Republican donor. Among other big investors in small ethanol companies: Microsoft founder Bill Gates and the politically connected Carlyle Group private equity firm, where George H. W. Bush was once a director. The 10 largest ethanol producers and their trade groups have handed out $4.7 million in federal campaign contributions [between 2000 and early 2007], says the Center for Responsive Politics. The Renewable Fuels Association has increased its lobbying spending 60 percent in the past seven years, and former Sens. Bob Dole of Kansas and Tom Daschle of South Dakota tout ethanol's national security benefits for a group of farm and energy interests called the 21st Century Agriculture Policy Project. Just as crucial, while far less tangible, has been Washington's veneration of the long-suffering small farmer, now turned ethanol entrepreneur.

It all paid off in 2005, when, with gasoline prices ratcheting higher, Congress wrote into its big energy bill a renewable fuel standard, an unprecedented mandate requiring refiners to double the amount of ethanol they blend into the nation's gasoline by 2012—a major coup for the industry. Congress's decision in that bill not to give the oil industry any protection from MTBE lawsuits made ethanol even hotter. Oil refiners immediately announced a switch to ethanol en masse, dramatically boosting demand.

Ethanol has proved one of the few issues in Washington for which it's nearly impossible to find a sparring partner.

Energy economist Philip Verleger is one of many who traced last summer's [2006] high gasoline prices to ethanol panic. As it turned out, the taxpayer paid twice. First, at the pump. Then, because of the long-standing ethanol tax breaks—now at 51 cents per gallon—the government sent $2.5 billion last year to the flush oil industry to blend ethanol it would have needed anyway.

Congress and the Demand for Ethanol

In 2006, production exceeded Congress's renewable fuel standard mandate by 25 percent, reaching 5 billion gallons produced. Nearly half of the gasoline being sold in the United States now contains 10 percent ethanol. But that leaves half the market open to conquest. Some 76 ethanol refineries are now under construction, including in such unlikely states as New York and Oregon, adding to the 112 already squeezing fuel from corn. By some counts, 200 more have been proposed.

Of course, oil prices—[which fell from August 2006 to February 2007]—could rain on the parade. In fact, Wall Street is so worried that cheaper petroleum will cool ethanol profitability, as it has in the past, that the stock prices of companies that went public with fanfare last summer [2006], VeraSun and Aventine, of Pekin, Ill., have slid 40 percent and 60 percent, respectively. Bill Gates would be $140 million richer if he had sold his stake in Pacific Ethanol of Fresno, Calif., when gas prices began to spike [during spring 2006]. As it stands, he's doing a bit better than break-even because of the bounce his company took after President [George W.] Bush made his pitch in the State of the Union address to increase renewable fuels—a universe now almost entirely made of ethanol—a staggering sevenfold by 2017. Congress is already on the case: All eyes are on the important farm bill being shepherded forward this year [2007] by Iowa Sen. Tom Harkin, chair of the Agriculture Committee, as the perfect vehicle to force increased ethanol demand on the market.

Indeed, ethanol has proved one of the few issues in Washington for which it's nearly impossible to find a sparring partner. Even Sen. John McCain, who gave up on Iowa in his 2000 presidential bid because of his opposition to ethanol subsidies, now says the fuel should be "carefully examined." Sen. Hillary Rodham Clinton, who once voted against the mandate, is calling for $1 billion in ethanol research.

There are ways ethanol can be a boon to the environment, there are ways that it could be a disaster for the environment, and the devil's in the details.

Food or Fuel?

A new ethanol surge could cause more problems than it solves. Last year's [2006] astounding growth in ethanol gobbled up 20 percent of the U.S. corn crop. That surpasses all the corn Americans consumed last year—whether in cereal, corn-syrup-sweetened soda, or on the cob. And the strain has become severe on the nation's primary use of corn—as feed for dairy and beef cattle, pigs, and chickens. Meat, dairy, and egg producers are reeling from corn prices that have doubled [between 2006 and 2007. By February 2007 corn was] trading above $4 a bushel for the first time in more than a decade.

The impact may really be felt when meat prices take off at the start of this summer's [2007] grilling season. "The American consumer is making a choice here," says Dick Bond, chief executive of Tyson Foods. "This is either corn for feed or corn for fuel." He indicated his company intends to be active in the farm bill debate on Capitol Hill, and some livestock groups recently wrote a letter to warn the secretary of agriculture of their concerns. Lester Brown of the Earth Policy Institute warns that ethanol is on track to consume half of the U.S. corn crop as early as 2008. He is calling for a moratorium on new refineries, similar to the one the world's No. 3 ethanol producer, China, announced in December [2006]. "We used to have a food economy and an energy economy," says Brown. "The two are merging. We need to . . . think through carefully what we're doing."

Ethanol's boosters are confident farmers will plant more acres and increase the yield of corn per acre, with the help of new seed and genetic engineering technology—easing the price pressure. But for now, the futures market shows corn prices climbing further. That's despite the fact that farmers are on track to plant 88 million acres of corn this year [2007]—up to 10 million over 2006 and more than has been planted in the United States at any time since the 1940s, when crop yields were a fraction of today's.

At What Cost to the Environment?

The frenzy for the new yellow gold is not without environmental consequences, either. Plenty of greenhouse-gas emitting fossil fuels are used to produce ethanol—tractors in the field, trucks on the road, and nitrogen-based fertilizer born of natural gas. Some say that ethanol actually uses more energy than it returns. But only one oft-quoted study arrived at this conclusion by using apparently obsolete data. A Congressional Research Service analysis [in 2006] concluded that "most studies give corn-based ethanol a slightly positive energy balance." A tepid endorsement, at best. On climate issues, researchers are concerned with ethanol's reliance on natural gas or coal throughout the production process. "Overall benefits in terms of . . . greenhouse gases are limited," concludes CRS. That problem may get worse with the emergence of coal-fired ethanol plants, like one that opened [in January 2007] in Richardton, N.D. Bob Dinneen of the Renewable Fuels Association points out relatively clean natural gas is the industry standard, and he believes more earth-friendly plants are the next wave, such as those that trap methane from cattle feedlots to fire their boilers. But without mandated emissions caps, refineries may have little incentive to invest in such costly technology.

Farmers most likely will grow their corn on acres they normally would have rotated to soybeans. But that zaps topsoil of nutrients while exacerbating pest problems and use of more fertilizers and insecticides, which can wind up in the water supply. Plus, some land currently held fallow in the Conservation Reserve Program is likely to be put back to work. The complex issues throw environmentalists into a briar patch. "I hate talking about ethanol," says Dan Becker, head of the Sierra Club's global warming program. "There are ways ethanol can be a boon to the environment, there are ways that it could be a disaster for the environment, and the devil's in the details."

Thanks to such loopholes and foot dragging on improvement in CAFE standards, average new vehicle efficiency has dropped since 1988.

Perhaps nothing illustrates the limits of an ethanol-fueled future better than the push for E-85—a mix that is 85 percent ethanol and 15 percent gasoline. It's available in only 1,000 of the nation's 180,000 gas stations, and Big Oil-branded stations haven't been quick to offer E-85. Ethanol boosters are hoping independent gas stations will step in, but it's costly. Trying to expand E-85's availability, the House is likely to pass a bill [in 2007] that will direct federal agencies to figure how to make the switchover more cheaply. Rep. Bart Gordon, chair of the House Science and Technology Committee, said such a move is necessary "if this country is serious about reducing our dependence on foreign oil."

Congress has been far more tentative in dealing with bigger delivery questions. No pipelines exist to move ethanol from the Midwest the way that gasoline is pumped out of the Gulf Coast; rail works well now to transport most ethanol, but 25 percent moves by truck (burning diesel petroleum along the way). As production increases, the transportation strain is sure to worsen.

Congress's Perverse Incentive

And even if E-85 were widely available tomorrow, it could be pumped only into the 2.5 percent of the nation's cars that are flexible fuel vehicles. Automakers have pledged to churn out many more, but Congress created a perverse incentive allowing them to produce more gas guzzlers if they manufacture enough flex fuel ears. Carmakers earned enough of a break on their Corporate Average Fuel Economy Standards that the nation will burn 17 billion more gallons of gasoline from 2001 to 2008 as a result.

Thanks to such loopholes and foot dragging on improvement in CAFE standards, average new vehicle efficiency has dropped since 1988—a problem that comes home to roost with ethanol. Because of its lower energy content, it takes 1.5 gallons of ethanol to drive as far as 1 gallon of gasoline. *Consumer Reports* calculates E-85 ended up costing motorists about a dollar extra per gallon last year because of the need to buy more fuel. Renewable fuels lobbyist Dinneen points out that carmakers could solve the problem with improved engine technology. But with the fleet on U.S. roads now, and gasoline consumption continuing to creep upward, even today's incredible growth in ethanol production barely makes a dent in the nation's oil dependence. Ethanol now amounts to just 4.3 percent of gasoline sold by volume, and just 2.9 percent by energy content.

Ethanol has a role to play in making the nation's energy situation more reliable, . . . but it's not a panacea.

While corn-based ethanol production has room to grow, the industry acknowledges there's a ceiling—about 15 billion gallons yearly by most accounts, or three times the production in 2006. That's 20 billion gallons short of Bush's renewable fuels goal. Even with alternatives like natural gas vehicles, plug-in hybrids, or hydrogen cars, major advances in ethanol are necessary.

The Future of Ethanol

In the laboratory, so-called cellulosic ethanol can be wrung from fibrous materials like cornhusks and rice hulls, as well as fast-growing reedy crops that require little fertilizer or tending, like switch grass, and timber industry excess. This would ease reliance on edible grain and spread the economic benefits beyond corn communities. Another bonus: Biotech enzymes rather than heat energy would break down the cellulose to fuel, reducing greenhouse gases to a fraction of those produced by corn.

But it has never been tried commercially, and it's unlikely that the fuel will go from zero to 90 billion gallons in 10 years. Just to get to 1 billion gallons of ethanol production, the corn industry took 13 years. The government estimates the capital cost of cellulosic is very likely five times that of corn. The expense surely would be driven down if production scales up, but a "chicken and egg problem" exists, says Harkin. "Investors are not investing in cellulosic plants because there's no supply," he says. "And farmers are not planting switch grass or other energy crops because there's no market." He has pledged to "jump-start" both demand and supply with research money and loan guarantees in a new farm bill.

But it will take more than money for new cellulosic technology to substantially weaken the grip of the nation's oil addiction. Lee Lynd, Dartmouth College engineering professor and cellulosic pioneer, who founded Mascoma, a company that is building a pilot plant outside Rochester, N.Y., believes cellulosic will make "a much more limited contribution to energy supply" if behaviors don't change as well as technologies. Ethanol would make its greatest dent if Americans drove less and highly efficient cars were deployed widely, he says. Others agree. "Ethanol has a role to play in making the nation's energy situation more reliable," says economist Robert Wescott. "But it's not a panacea." That brings the debate back to the nitty-gritty fuel economy and conservation issues politicians have been mostly avoiding for years. They'd rather feel good, for the time being, about ethanol.

The Politics of Ethanol Are Driven by Special Interests

David S. Bullock

David S. Bullock is a professor at the University of Illinois at Urbana, Champaign in the Department of Agricultural and Consumer Economics. He has written numerous articles on the economic consequences of various agricultural policies.

As a political issue, America's ethanol policy is strongly influenced by various special interest groups that stand to gain or lose directly from changes in the way the federal government supports ethanol as an alternative fuel. The claims made by these groups in support of their policy arguments are often in conflict and often based on different sets of assumptions about the costs and benefits of ethanol policy. We can make better sense of the arguments surrounding ethanol by paying close attention to which groups actually bear the costs or reap the profits from any proposed change in policy. One important feature of ethanol subsidies is that they are much easier to put into place than they are to remove, making some policy decisions concerning ethanol effectively irreversible.

The United States is currently passing through one of the most exciting and controversial periods of its energy history. With the US military caught up in armed conflict in the Middle East, and with global warming looming in the minds

David S. Bullock, *Corn-Based Ethanol in Illinois and the U.S.: A Report from the Department of Agricultural and Consumer Economics, University of Illinois*, Urbana, IL: Farmdoc, University of Illinois at Urbana-Champaign, 2007. Reproduced by permission. http://www.farmdoc.uiuc.edu.

of many expert scientists as the world's greatest environmental challenge, a common belief is that it is more important than ever that the US develop sensible and far-sighted energy policy.

Special Interests vs. the Common Good

Politicians' claims aside, the politics of energy policy are rarely about what is best "for the country." When government sets energy policy, some people gain, and others may lose. The politics of energy policy, then, are not simply, or even generally, about how to make the nation as a whole better off. Rather, the politics of energy policy are very much about interested political groups struggling against one another. This type of "special interest" politics is nothing new, and not unique to energy policy. Nevertheless, it is widely held among average Americans that the political activities of special interest politics are often bad for the nation as a whole. . . .

Who owns the farmland is of ultimate importance in the analysis of the impacts of ethanol policy on income distribution.

Groups of citizens are interested in ethanol policy because their well-beings are affected by it, either positively or negatively. The special interest groups involved in the ethanol policy debate are several and varied, and they express several and varied political viewpoints. Claims made by different interest groups as to the benefits and costs of ethanol policy often are contradictory. To analyze these divergent claims, we first review what they are.

Arguments Made by Corn Growers

Clearly, the companies that produce ethanol are affected by and work to affect ethanol policy. This group is not homogeneous. It is comprised both of agribusiness giants, such as Archer Daniels Midland, and of smaller, farmer-owned cooperatives whose members have pooled their resources to invest in an industry that they hope adds value to their crops. Even such cooperatives are not homogeneous. Some of the members of these farmer-cooperatives are people of moderate means who have spent their lives mostly working others' land. Others are multi-millionaires owning thousands of acres of prime farmland worth thousands of dollars per acre.

An important organization through which ethanol producers represent themselves politically is the Renewable Fuels Association (RFA). The RFA's ethanol policy opinions and arguments are not difficult to find on the Internet:

> A Success Story: The federal ethanol program has been a tremendous success, helping to build a strong domestic energy resource. . . . Today, approximately 30% of the nation's gasoline is blended with ethanol—reducing the demand for imports, stimulating economic benefits across the country, and reducing air pollution. And the federal government realizes a net gain annually due to increased tax revenues and reduced farm program costs.

Because of the current political popularity of the ethanol industry, the [American Petroleum Institute] has been careful not to express overtly anti-ethanol political arguments.

In the US, corn is the chief input to ethanol production. When government policies encourage ethanol production, they raise demand for corn, which raises the price of corn. There is no doubt that ethanol policy was a key factor leading to the high corn prices of 2006 and 2007. Corn farmers, then, also take interest in ethanol policy, and their organizations participate actively in ethanol politics. As do many interest groups, sometimes corn farmer organizations like to argue that policies that favor them also favor the citizenry in general:

NCGA [National Corn Growers Association] believes it is in the best interest of the US consumer to have a comprehensive National Energy Plan, which includes renewable fuels. Renewable fuels will provide an environmentally clean, domestically produced fuel, which will contribute to our independence from foreign oil. In addition, rural communities benefit from the additional jobs created through the development of this renewable fuel industry.

But again, corn farmers are not a homogeneous group. Especially important to this study is that some corn farmers own much farmland while others own little.

Many times US citizens have sided with foreign interest groups, participating in a "food versus fuel" debate in their attempts to affect US ethanol policy.

In addition, many owners of farmland are not farmers at all. Often, they are the widows or descendants of one-time farmers, who live in cities and act as absentee landlords. Some farmland owners are wealthy individuals and corporations who simply own agricultural land as an investment in their large portfolios. Some are real estate developers waiting to turn farmland on the outskirts of cities into housing developments and shopping malls. We will argue that who owns the farmland is of ultimate importance in the analysis of the impacts of ethanol policy on income distribution. Ethanol policy allows landlords to raise the rental rates of their land, which must be paid by those who actually farm it. It is not at all clear, therefore, that when ethanol policy raises the price of corn, that it benefits all "family farmers." Surely it benefits those families that own a lot of farmland, some of whom actually farm that farmland. It may harm those farmers who rent their land from absentee landlords.

Arguments Made by Oil Companies
and Cattle Farmers

Ethanol competes with gasoline for American motorists' dollars. Therefore members of the petroleum industry also maintain interests in ethanol policy. The petroleum industry is not homogeneous, either. Rather it is comprised of many different firms at many different levels. Multinational conglomerates, such as Exxon/Mobil, dwarf even the agri-business giants. These companies explore and drill for crude oil, buy crude oil from foreign nations, transport crude oil around the world, refine it into motor fuel and other products, transport motor fuel around the US by pipeline, distribute it to local service stations, and sell it to consumers. Other, smaller companies also compete in the petroleum industry: owners of small crude oil reserves in Texas and Oklahoma, independent refineries and distribution terminals, independent truckers, and of course owners of service station franchises. All such entities take an interest in ethanol policy, and many are active in ethanol politics. A main representative organization of the petroleum industry is the American Petroleum Institute (API). Because of the current political popularity of the ethanol industry, recently the API has been careful not to express overtly anti-ethanol political arguments, but rather has emphasized that market forces should determine economic outcomes. . . .

Not all those whom we generally consider to be farmers benefit from ethanol policy. In particular, farmers who produce livestock, and buy corn to feed their livestock, increasingly have felt harmed by the high corn prices brought about by ethanol policy. Recently livestock producers' organizations have been less reticent than has the API to state their true views of ethanol policy [as evidenced by this quote from Paul Hitch, president of the National Cattlemen's Beef Association]:

This ethanol binge is insane. This talk about energy independence and wrapping yourself in the flag and singing "God Bless America"—all that's going to come at a severe cost to another part of the economy.

Arguments Concerning Food Prices

US ethanol policy can affect commodity prices in the rest of the world. As a result, many citizens of other countries take interests in US ethanol policy, and participate in the US policy debate. Many times US citizens have sided with foreign interest groups, participating in a "food versus fuel" debate in their attempts to affect US ethanol policy. Tortilla prices in Mexico have skyrocketed over the past year. Recently [2007] Mexican consumers' protests over US ethanol policy have been in the spotlight. . . .

US corn growers' organizations have made counter-arguments [like this one from the National Corn Growers Association]:

> Skeptics suggest the corn industry will face difficulty in meeting demand and growers will experience a dilemma of whether to supply customers in the feed, food and export markets or to supply the burgeoning ethanol industry. This contrived "food versus fuel" argument is fraught with misguided logic, deception, and scare tactics. . . . Detractors argue that grain markets should adhere to a hierarchical approach that emphasizes grain's utility as food and feed. But what about the fundamental human needs of energy, security, and mobility? . . . MYTH: Ethanol production diverts corn away from food and feed markets. FACT: There will be plenty of corn available.

Environmental Arguments on Both Sides

Environmental concerns have been a key focus of the ethanol policy debate. Not surprisingly, pro-ethanol interest groups [such as the Renewable Fuels Association] have argued that ethanol is good for the environment:

Ethanol is one of the best tools we have to fight air pollution from vehicles. Ethanol contains 35% oxygen. Adding oxygen to fuel results in more complete fuel combustion, thus reducing harmful tailpipe emissions. Ethanol also displaces the use of toxic gasoline components such as benzene, a carcinogen. Ethanol is non-toxic, water soluble and quickly biodegradable.

But some environmental groups have been skeptical of such claims. The following appeared in the Sierra Club's *Sierra* magazine:

Supporters tout ethanol as "renewable," but it takes the equivalent of 70 percent of the energy in a gallon of ethanol to fertilize, harvest, transport, and distill it. (Efficiency like that could give renewability a bad name.) Senator Dianne Feinstein (D-Calif.) called the proposal a "wealth transfer" to corn-producing states from the rest of the country, but she and other dissenters were overwhelmed by farm-state senators of both parties, as well as the recipients of campaign largesse from Archer Daniels Midland. . . .

At the same time that pro-ethanol interest groups and politicians focus on claims that the ethanol subsidies benefit consumers and independent gasoline marketers, however, they also claim that current pro-ethanol policies are crucial to the family farm.

Additionally, various scientists have questioned the environmental and health benefits of current ethanol policy. Commenting on his recently published academic article, Stanford University atmospheric scientist Mark Jacobson stated,

Ethanol is being promoted as a clean and renewable fuel that will reduce global warming and air pollution, but our results show that a high blend of ethanol poses an equal or greater risk to public health than gasoline, which already causes significant health damage.

Arguments About Who Benefits

Arguments about who pays taxes and who receives subsidies abound in the political rhetoric that surrounds ethanol policy. For example, the National Corn Growers Association has stated on its web site,

> ... fuel blended with 10 percent ethanol receives a tax credit of 5.1 cents per gallon. E-85, which is 85 percent ethanol by volume, receives a 43-cent-per-gallon credit. Petroleum blenders—not corn farmers—receive this tax credit. . . .

The ethanol policy debate is contentious and complicated, and often not completely honest.

At the same time that pro-ethanol interest groups and politicians focus on claims that the ethanol subsidies benefit consumers and independent gasoline marketers, however, they also claim that current pro-ethanol policies are crucial to the family farm. Even the most conservative anti-tax/anti-government-spending politicians [such as Pat Buchanan] have seen fit to make these claims:

> ... Just as I support the independence of the family farm, I support a policy of US energy independence that includes a strong stand for ethanol. This industry creates 40,000 jobs, adds $12 billion in net farm income each year. . . .

But politicians from outside the Corn Belt [such as Sen. John McCain of Arizona] often feel quite differently:

> ... It's hard to justify continued government subsidies for programs that haven't lived up to expectations after more than two decades of government assistance. . . . It's even harder when those subsidies are given to an industry that makes over $30 million a year producing ethanol.

Taxes and Security

Ultimately, ethanol policy can affect the prices consumers pay for motor fuel, and much ethanol policy is paid for through taxes. To some degree, the "average American," represented by organized consumer and taxpayer groups [such as Taxpayers for Common Sense], has also participated in the politics of ethanol:

> Instead of supporting the traditional American farmer and reducing our oil demands, ethanol subsidies are a corporate handout to big agribusiness disguised as fuel innovation.

Perhaps even more importantly, the average American has an interest in the degree to which the country is energy-independent. It is widely held that the nation's dependence on foreign oil has contributed to its involvement in the Middle East's political conflicts. It is obvious that this involvement has been costly, not only to the US Treasury, but also to the individuals and families, both American and foreign, hurt by military conflict and terrorism.

The quotations provided above make it clear that the ethanol policy debate is contentious and complicated, and often not completely honest. Different groups, from the Midwest to the Middle East, are working, sometimes for the common good and sometimes in their own special interests, to influence US ethanol policy. These groups have much to gain and much to lose from ethanol policy, as well as much to reveal and much to hide in ethanol politics. Indeed, the nation as a whole has much to gain from sound ethanol policy, and much to lose from poor ethanol policy. . . .

Subsidies Are a Political Ratchet

Another question is how flexible factors [of ethanol production] are in moving *out* of ethanol production and into an alternative use. It is crucial for policy makers to understand this concept and its implications. Some factors are reasonably flexible—the transportation trucks and rail cars can be moved to alternative activities with relative ease. But other factors are considerably less flexible. It would be difficult to move some forms of labor and know-how out of the sector, especially in any kind of short run. Ethanol factories are built in rural communities, and thus one of the political justifications for providing subsidies to ethanol is to create factory jobs in rural areas. If workers and managers own homes in a small town, then when an ethanol plant shuts down it may be impossible for them to sell their homes without a huge loss in equity, and therefore they may not be able to get out of the town that they moved into earlier, when they anticipated that ethanol markets would remain strong, and government policy would remain favorable, for many years to come. Even less flexible are the buildings and machines that make up the ethanol plant itself. Clearly it is not generally feasible to move the buildings. And many of the machines used in an ethanol plant are not very useful in other industries.

This irreversibility of bringing factors into ethanol production causes the subsidy policy to act like a political ratchet. It is easy enough politically to cause the subsidy to go up: corn farmers and ethanol producers influence their congressional representatives, and everyone refers to energy self-sufficiency and rural job creation. But once in place, it may well become politically infeasible to bring the subsidy back down. For, after the economy is finished building new ethanol factories, in response to the subsidy, what then? We've already argued that when the building process is through, many ethanol factories will not be making large profits. The factories and their workers, then, would be quite vulnerable if, for example, any of the following transpired: 1) the government decided to remove or lower the subsidy, 2) world oil prices fell and remained low for an extended period, and/or 3) droughts led to poor corn harvests in consecutive years. In any such circumstance, it will be extremely difficult for government to tell factories that are losing money and workers who are losing jobs, "Sorry, but that's the free market." Rather, it will be politically expedient to raise subsidization levels. Thus, a major concern is that ethanol subsidies are relatively easy for governments to get into, but very difficult for governments to get out of.

9

The Government's Promotion of Corn-Based Ethanol Must Be Reexamined

Kiran Bhat

Kiran Bhat is a staff writer at the Harvard International Review, *a quarterly journal of international affairs published by the Harvard International Relations Council.*

United States government support for the ethanol industry through subsidies is misguided given that the benefits of ethanol are not as great as its proponents maintain. The effect of ethanol consumption on food prices in other parts of the world—particularly in the world's poorest countries—and the questionable environmental benefits of ethanol use indicate that it is not in our interests to spend as much as we do on ethanol. Because it would be very difficult politically to remove existing subsidies, U.S. policy may need to focus on other solutions such as greater fuel efficiency and research for alternative sources of energy.

When the state of Iowa becomes a priority in the US presidential election, it is only a matter of time before agriculture dominates the discussion. Indeed, US presidential candidates Hillary Clinton, John McCain, and Barack Obama all brought out their metaphorical overalls to sing praises of corn farmers before the February [2008] caucuses. Such kowtowing to Iowa's farmers has become a quadrennial tradition in the United States, where federal corn subsidies totaled

Kiran Bhat, "Misplaced Priorities: Ethanol Promotion and Its Unintended Consequences," *Harvard International Review*, Spring 2008, p. 30–33. Copyright © 2008 The Harvard International Review. Reproduced by permission.

US$37.3 billion from 1995 to 2003. The United States' funding of corn farmers stems largely from precedent, a desire to keep the heartland happy, and perhaps even a romanticized conception of small farmers. However, the subsidies also have significant roots in one of the most confounding environmental programs of the past 30 years: ethanol fuel.

After considering corn-derived ethanol's questionable status as an energy-efficient fuel, ... US government policies in support of ethanol look fundamentally unsound.

According to the *Economist*, over 200 distinct subsidy programs provide US$7 billion each year to participants in all levels of ethanol production and supply. Since the 1970s, untold billions in handouts have been given to corn farmers, "big ethanol" refining companies such as Archer Daniels Midland, and gas stations in an effort to boost ethanol's profile in the US market. And if federal subsidies to all parties involved in the production of ethanol were not enough, the US government currently places a US$0.54 per gallon tariff on imported ethanol. Several state governments have started subsidy programs as well. This amount of market protection is inordinate for a fuel whose true value—without government support—seems low.

The Questionable Benefits of Ethanol

While subsidies are often perceived to be good for US business, the magnitude of government handouts to corn farmers in the United States produces pernicious consequences around the world. Government actions have artificially increased US demand for corn, driving up the prevailing world price of corn by over 50 percent since 2006. While rising world food costs are not the fault of the US ethanol regime alone, support for ethanol does play a significant role in rising prices. This effect is especially dire for poor countries accustomed to years of falling food costs. In addition to its direct implications on the world food market, ethanol—touted by US policymakers as a solid source of renewable energy—may not be a viable alternate fuel. There remain practical concerns to its implementation, and there is no consensus on the fuel's environmental benefit.

After considering corn-derived ethanol's questionable status as an energy-efficient fuel, along with the unintended food price blowback of its subsidization, US government policies in support of ethanol look fundamentally unsound. While political realities may not allow for the removal of distorting subsidies, the US government may eventually realize that money should shift from the production of ethanol itself toward research being conducted to make the existing industry more efficient. If ethanol production technologies are streamlined, less corn would be needed to produce the same amount of product. This would eliminate the need for subsidies, which are in part causing rising food prices and nearly eliminating ethanol's environmental benefits.

Corn prices rose 50 percent from 2006 levels, and wheat prices more than doubled in price per ton. Blind promotion of ethanol is at least partially to blame for these increases.

Hungry for Fuel, Hungry for Food

The hype surrounding ethanol raises concern about the dangerous and increasing integration between energy markets and agriculture. Demand for food products now depends not just on the literal hunger and nutritional consumption of humans, but also on a "hunger" for energy. This growing connection has an underlying moral dilemma; is it fair to produce fuel from food that otherwise could have been used for nourishment? The answer to this question is debatable, and largely unclear.

Some other, more pragmatic economic questions have empirical answers. Data shows that mixing energy and agriculture markets has severe policy blowback, affecting consumers at home to the developing world's poor. As prices of corn have risen from subsidies, so have the prices of its grain substitutes—wheat, barley, and others. Processed foods that use the grains as staples have also increased in price, a result which hits foreign and US consumers squarely in the pocketbook. Consumers worldwide are increasingly angry: in early 2007, Mexico City faced riots over the doubling in prices of corn-based tortillas.

C. Ford Runge and Benjamin Senauer, professors of applied economics at the University of Minnesota, noted in their 2007 article in *Foreign Affairs* that "biofuels have tied oil and food prices together in ways that could profoundly upset the relationships between food producers, consumers, and nations in the years ahead, with potentially devastating implications for both global poverty and food security." The same article also cites figures which indicate that continuing high oil prices (which are likely, considering the ongoing conflicts in the Middle East), would raise corn prices by 41 percent by 2020. Given overall food price increases, the number of "chronically hungry" people in the world could also rise to 1.2 billion by the same year.

While some data indicates that ethanol already is, or is at least becoming, more energy efficient, there is still no scientific consensus on whether it is good for the environment.

Food price increases are most devastating for the world's poorest consumers. Congress' desire to establish a functional ethanol infrastructure through subsidies has increased food prices to the point that farmers in sub-Saharan Africa, Asia, and Latin America are often unable to afford feed for their farm animals. Poor consumers are simply unable to afford food for themselves and their families. Small price increases could starve poor families in the lesser-developed world, and the price increases driven in part by the ethanol craze are much larger than marginal. Over the course of last year [2007], corn prices rose 50 percent from 2006 levels, and wheat prices more than doubled in price per ton. Blind promotion of ethanol is at least partially to blame for these increases.

A Questionable Environmental Solution

Although its distortionary effect on the world food market is immediate and palpable, ethanol also runs counter to environmental sensibilities. There is no consensus on whether it is even an efficient, viable alternative fuel source. US ethanol is derived from domestically grown corn, which requires fossil fuels to harvest and ship to refineries. Similarly, as the final ethanol liquid product cannot be transported through pipelines because it requires absolute purity and low water levels, additional fossil fuels are required to transport ethanol to gas stations on trucks, barges, and trains.

Some research has found that ethanol is efficient overall in that more energy is created by ethanol fuel than is used to produce it. According to a *BusinessWeek* report, scientists at a lab funded by the US Department of Energy have found that ethanol delivers about 1 million British Thermal Units (BTUs) of energy for every 0.74 million BTUs of fossil fuel consumed. Gasoline, in contrast, consumes 1.23 million BTUs of fossil fuel for every 1 million BTUs delivered. These results are corroborated by a 2006 National Academy of Sciences study, which found an equivalent 25 percent positive net energy balance for corn grain ethanol. As time goes on, ethanol production should slowly become more efficient in terms of net energy balance, as has been the trend over the past few decades. Cellulose-based ethanol, which is derived from a biomaterial found in most plants, is considered to be a more energy efficient version of corn ethanol. It is currently being promoted as a more environmentally friendly, efficient alternative.

A confluence of political interests has pushed the ethanol project on the United States in place of cheaper, more convenient and less distortionary alternatives.

While some data indicates that ethanol already is, or is at least becoming, more energy efficient, there is still no scientific consensus on whether it is good for the environment. Some choose to focus less on energy efficiency and more on the carbon emissions that result from ethanol's production and use. Robert Bryce, a fellow at the Institute for Energy Research, claims, "Virtually all studies show that greenhouse gases associated with ethanol and gasoline are about the same once the entire life cycle of the two fuels are compared."

Even if ethanol can be considered more environmentally friendly than gasoline, it still remains to be asked whether it can even be practically introduced as viable replacement for gasoline. The answer to this question is much clearer. If the United States were to depend entirely on domestic crop reserves for ethanol for energy, demand would outstrip supply to such a degree that even if the entire biomass of the United States were used to produce ethanol, there would still be an energy shortage. Tad Patzek, an environmental and civil engineering professor at the University of California, Berkeley, noted in remarks to the National Press Club in 2005 that "compared with current energy use in the United States, the impact of biomass is almost negligible, regardless of its source."

Patzek asserts that there are several alternatives to funding the ethanol behemoth that would probably help the environment more than the increasingly prevalent use of mixed ethanol and gasoline, or "gasahol." The first is to ensure that car tires are properly inflated, and the second is to increase fuel efficiency of today's vehicles by just three to five miles per gallon. Patzek also suggests investment in solar energy, which "is at least 100 times more efficient in delivering work than corn ethanol." Even if ethanol is energy efficient, it will never be able to replace gasoline as the United States' main source of fuel. As Patzek makes clear, many different types of measures and alternate energy sources could more significantly reduce humans' impact on the environment at a lower cost than the continued rollout of ethanol.

The notable feature of Patzek's alternatives is that each one is much more pragmatic than the construction of the new ethanol-based fuel infrastructure. An outside observer would think that these low-cost, convenient, and environmentally friendlier alternatives would gain predominance. Strangely enough, however, a confluence of political interests has pushed the ethanol project on the United States in place of cheaper, more convenient and less distortionary alternatives.

A Political Phenomenon

Ethanol has achieved success as an alternative fuel largely because it is a convenient policy point for politicians. Corn is a big industry in the Midwest, where presidential nominations are often secured. At the same time, the opposition to ethanol is disorganized, quiet, and politically insignificant. Therefore, politicians have found that supporting ethanol is truly a risk-free political proposition that ensures the support of the thousands invested in the industry without any political downside.

In truth, the ethanol "industry" is not so much determined by market forces as it is by political concerns.

Ethanol is also popular because it tangentially appeals to people of different ideologies and backgrounds. Environmentalists view ethanol as one of the key potential clean fuels of the future. Neoconservatives, who are often at the other end of the political spectrum, see it as a potential way to end the addiction to Middle-Eastern oil and therefore increase the US' relative power standing. Farmers perceive it as a means of earning government money, while suburbanites and urbanites see it as a way to reduce guilt over ruining the environment with gasoline. The issue thus has a broad, if not very deep, appeal to most significant political demographics in the country.

The fuss over ethanol is also peculiar because it may have never emerged had it not been for the 1973 OPEC oil embargo. OPEC's decision to withhold oil due to US support of Israel during the Yom Kippur War forced then US President [Jimmy] Carter to address increasing concerns over energy dependence. In 1977, Carter called for a plan to use US domestic resources to serve the nation's own energy needs and stressed the importance of finding new sources of fuel. Ethanol fit the bill and first gained policy backing in 1980, when Carter approved an election-year subsidy of US$340 million to ethanol production factories in the Midwest. President Ronald Reagan, the famed small government conservative, followed suit—his Department of Agriculture gave US$70 million in government-funded corn to ethanol production companies for free in 1987.

Just as political circumstance aided the initial emergence of ethanol decades ago, such circumstance continues to support ethanol today. President [George W.] Bush's call in the 2007 State of the Union for Congress to pass laws promoting renewable fuels is almost universally popular and has given a boost to ethanol. In December 2007, Congress passed the Energy Independence and Security Act, which requires that 36 billion gallons of alternative fuel be used by 2022. Current ethanol production is at 7.8 billion gallons a year, and although other renewable fuels are included in the 36 billion gallon figure, the bill still mandates a large increase in ethanol production.

As a result, the industry continues to grow unhindered. The Renewable Fuel Association's 2008 Ethanol Outlook Report notes that 2007 saw the introduction of 29 new operational ethanol refineries and a 2 billion gallon increase in ethanol production. In 2008, 68 refineries will either be expanding capacity or beginning production, which will result in a forecasted 6 billion gallon increase in production. These increases in production will command an increase in government subsidies propping up the entire program.

Since the ethanol craze is linked to political convenience, support for the program may fluctuate with ethanol's ability to bring in votes in the Midwest.

The ethanol industry is in place today because of a series of political circumstances that spawned government mandates on ethanol content in fuel, as well as subsidies to farmers and producers. In truth, the ethanol "industry" is not so much determined by market forces as it is by political concerns. Before changing his position on ethanol ahead of the Iowa primaries, John McCain correctly wrote in a letter to President Bush concerning ethanol legislation that the fuel "is a product that would not exist if Congress didn't create an artificial market for it."

Therein lies a primary problem with ethanol—it has developed entirely as a political phenomenon and as such is blindly promoted. Because it has not been tested in the open market, ethanol has emerged as the US' favorite alternative fuel without much examination of its viability as a source of clean, efficient, renewable energy.

Ethanol's Future

The one way to immediately end some of the distortive effects that subsidies have had on food prices is to remove the protections themselves. If the United States were to import ethanol from Brazil, where infrastructure for the production and distribution of sugarcane-based ethanol is already established, it would be able to achieve many of the same goals without taking food off the tables of the foreign poor. But considering the disproportionate strength of the US farm lobby, and the predominant political desire for energy independence rather than just energy sustainability, the removal of US subsidies will not happen any time soon.

Still, since the ethanol craze is linked to political convenience, support for the program may fluctuate with ethanol's ability to bring in votes in the Midwest. As the election year passes into memory, the US government may begin to shift its priority away from the physical production of ethanol toward research on the development of new, more efficient methods of production. Currently, subsidies to corn farmers are politically expedient. But once the influence of Iowa fades and the next administration needs a political victory, attention may turn to tangible progress on the energy front. There, the US government may find an opening to shift priorities from physical production toward research. This simple change would promote efficiency, environmental friendliness, and global conscientiousness in the ethanol industry. If ethanol production becomes significantly more efficient as the result of new research on the cellulose model, ethanol may actually become environmentally and commercially viable. Theoretically then, no subsidies of a particular plant would be necessary nor would there be such a considerable rise in world food prices.

But if for political or practical reasons such a shift in priorities does not occur, the US government will focus on simpler, more pragmatic complements to ethanol. Such measures could include significant increases in mileage standards in cars, or greater grant funding for more efficient sources of energy such as solar power. Although these efforts do little to fix ethanol's problems, they could buttress the country's attempts to achieve energy independence and a new, reliable renewable fuel. Such outcomes would indirectly reduce the power that the ethanol industry currently wields.

In the world of renewable energy, there is no panacea. Ethanol, which had originally seemed so promising, has taken its share of criticism over the past few years. But its emergence marks a commitment to renewable fuels, even if the commitment is mostly driven by the desire for energy independence. It is necessary to translate that commitment into a smart, feasible, and fair reality that helps the world more than it harms it. Hopefully, when the US presidential election season ends, the winning candidate will have the political will (and capital) to put away those metaphorical farmer overalls, and work toward that goal.

10

Government Subsidies for Corn-Based Ethanol Production Are Ineffective

Jerry Taylor and Peter Van Doren

Jerry Taylor and Peter Van Doren are senior fellows at the Cato Institute, a nonprofit public-policy research foundation dedicated to the libertarian principles of limited government, free markets, and individual liberty. Peter Van Doren is also editor of the quarterly journal Regulation, *which provides in-depth analysis of federal government regulations.*

Ethanol production in America has been supported for decades by staggering public subsidies without which there would be no justification for producing ethanol from corn at all. Although it is commonly argued that subsidies for ethanol are necessary to make it competitive with subsidized oil, oil subsidies are in reality quite modest. Because ethanol is not economically feasible without subsidies, and the environmental benefits of ethanol are largely fictional, our current ethanol policy amounts to no more than a transfer of wealth from taxpayers generally to owners of agricultural land.

The closest thing to a state religion in America today isn't Christianity—it's corn. Whether liberal or conservative, Democrat or Republican, urban or rural, virtually everyone in the business of offering opinions is in firm and total agreement that America's ills, from Islamic terrorism to global

Jerry Taylor and Peter Van Doren, "The Ethanol Boondoggle" *The Milken Institute Review*, First Quarter 2007. Reproduced by permission. http://www.cato.org/pubs/articles/ethanol-boondoggle.pdf.

warming to economic stagnation in the heartland, could be solved by a hefty dose of 200-proof grain alcohol.

Virtually everyone, however, does not include economists worthy of their No Free Lunch buttons. To them, the dizzying array of federal, state and local subsidies, preferences and mandates for ethanol fuel are a sad reflection of how a mix of cynical politics and we-can-do-anything American naiveté can cloud minds and distort markets. If ethanol had economic merit, no government assistance would be needed. Investors would pour money into the ethanol business and profits would be made, even as alcohol displaced oil in the markets for liquid fuels.

Without . . . subsidies, there would be no corn-based ethanol production at all. . . . The stuff only makes it to the pump because the feds and the states give it a big financial boost.

The Magnitude of Subsidies

If ethanol lacks economic merit, however, no amount of subsidy is likely to provide it. And make no mistake—welfare directed now (and for many decades) at the ethanol industry is staggering. A comprehensive study recently published by the nonpartisan International Institute for Sustainable Development estimates that federal and state subsidies for ethanol in 2006 were somewhere between $5.1 billion and $6.8 billion, and that they will soon increase, to as much as $8.7 billion annually, assuming no further change in policy.

Those estimates, moreover, are conservative, because they do not include the benefits bestowed by federal and state ethanol-consumption mandates, loan guarantees, subsidized loans, implicit subsidies provided by tax-exempt bond financing for the construction of ethanol processing plants, subsidized water for corn production, and state vehicle-purchase incentives. Don't forget the regulatory loophole given to manufacturers of flex-fueled vehicles—cars that can run on gasoline or blends of gasoline and ethanol—under federal automobile fuel-efficiency mandates.

Oil subsidies may generate modest windfalls for corporations in the oil business and their employees, but they do not have a noticeable effect on oil prices.

Without those subsidies, there would be no corn-based ethanol production at all. According to the U.S. Department of Agriculture, corn ethanol's variable production costs are 96 cents a gallon, while capital costs average $1.57. The upshot is that ethanol costs an average of $2.53 a gallon to produce in the United States, far more than the cost of conventional gasoline. The stuff only makes it to the pump because the feds and the states give it a big financial boost. In 2006, the subsidies translated into $1.05 to $1.38 per gallon of ethanol, or 42 percent to 55 percent of its wholesale market price.

Proponents justify this marketing intervention with a number of arguments. Ethanol subsidies, we are told:

- Level the playing field, which is distorted by subsidies to the oil industry. . . .

- Promote cleaner-burning fuel, which, in turn, improves air quality and reduces greenhouse gas emissions.

- Provide an economic stimulus to rural America by creating jobs and income that would otherwise not exist.

Close examination reveals that these are flimsy rationales for the real purpose of the program—to convince urban voters and their representatives to willingly hand over their money to corn farmers and the rapidly growing ranks of investors in ethanol plants.

Ethanol and the Unlevel Playing Field

Contrary to popular belief, federal oil subsidies are quite modest. When the Department of Energy examined those subsidies in 1999 (the most recent year in which a comprehensive analysis was performed), researchers found that they totaled a mere $567 million per year. That figure did not change significantly until passage of the 2005 Energy Policy Act, which added an estimated $1.4 billion of subsidies for the oil industry, spread out over a decade. So, while no comprehensive up-to-date assessment of federal oil subsidies is currently available, the 2006 total is certainly less than $1 billion—which translates to 0.3 cents per gallon of gasoline.

> One of the most commonly heard claims about ethanol is that it reduces automobile pollution. . . . Calling these claims the equivalent of the Big Lie is probably harsh, but it's also accurate.

More important for our purposes, however, is the fact that federal oil subsidies do not significantly affect gasoline prices. That's because U.S. oil prices are established in global crude oil markets, and subsidies to U.S. oil producers have little effect on global supply and demand. Oil subsidies may generate modest windfalls for corporations in the oil business and their employees, but they do not have a noticeable effect on oil prices and, thus, on the efficiency of energy markets.

Oil subsidies might reduce prices if they increased global oil supply by enough to affect global crude oil prices. But a Tufts University economist, Gilbert Metcalf, calculates that federal oil subsidies increase United States production by no more than 0.3 percent and that global prices are no more than 0.7 percent lower as a consequence.

In any case, the proper remedy for an objectionable subsidy is its elimination, not the imposition of a countervailing subsidy. The riposte that oil subsidies are impossible to eradicate, thus necessitating a "second-best" response of counter-subsidy—is hardly persuasive. Oil subsidies have been eliminated in the past—most recently, during the Reagan administration. . . .

Ethanol and the Environment

One of the most commonly heard claims about ethanol is that it reduces automobile pollution. Archer Daniels Midland, the gigantic commodities processor, has paid for an avalanche of advertising for some years now suggesting that ethanol is the thin yellow kernel standing between us and environmental Armageddon.

Calling these claims the equivalent of the Big Lie is probably harsh, but it's also accurate. The only thorough appraisal of the peer-reviewed and technical literature of which we are aware was published last year by Prof. Robert Niven of the Australian Defense Force Academy at the University of New South Wales. He found that when evaporative emissions are taken into account, E10 (fuel that's nine parts conventional gasoline to one part ethanol, the standard mix in service stations in the United States) actually increases emissions of total hydrocarbons, non-methane organic compounds and volatile toxins. Photo-chemical smog is worsened by ethanol consumption, while ambient concentrations of toxic chemicals are higher as well. By no coincidence, air pollution is even worse from E85, the 85 percent ethanol fuel now being heavily promoted by General Motors.

Although the environmental debate regarding ethanol is almost exclusively concerned with air-quality issues, a forgotten dimension concerns the effect of ethanol consumption on land use.

The picture is a bit better for greenhouse gas emissions, but not by much. Niven's review found that El0 offers only a 1 percent to 5 percent reduction of greenhouse emissions over conventional gasoline. The use of pure ethanol as a transportation fuel, however, as is used in Brazil, might reduce this category of emissions by up to 12 percent.

Note, though, that even this latter number is hard to pin down because of the larger disagreements about the energy needed to produce ethanol. Those who believe that ethanol production requires more fossil fuels—something has to power the tractors that till the fields, provide feed stocks for the chemical fertilizers and fire the boilers that distill the alcohol—than it actually generates, assert that ethanol has little impact on overall greenhouse gas emissions. Those who believe that ethanol has a positive net energy balance produce higher estimates for greenhouse gas savings. The debate surrounding ethanol's net energy balance is highly uncertain and data to settle the matter is not available.

In any event, this debate about life-cycle emissions from ethanol misses the point that reducing greenhouse gas emissions via ethanol would be an incredibly costly proposition—$250 per ton according to a recent report by the International Energy Agency. Moreover, that's a conservative estimate, because the agency considered only greenhouse gas emissions from automobile tailpipes. Given that most of the emissions associated with ethanol come from upstream in the production process, a full accounting would inflate its estimate dramatically.

Spending $250 (at the very least) to remove a ton of carbon from the atmosphere is an incredibly expensive way to get the job done—and one that surely costs more than it benefits the environment. William Nordhaus of Yale, for example, calculates that an optimal policy of greenhouse gas controls would embrace abatement costs of between $15 and $22 per ton of carbon in the United States. Accordingly, employing ethanol to reduce greenhouse gas emissions is fantastically wasteful.

Wait, it gets worse. Although the environmental debate regarding ethanol is almost exclusively concerned with air-quality issues, a forgotten dimension concerns the effect of ethanol consumption on land use. Profitable corn production requires tremendous amounts of fertilizer, pesticide and water. Increasing the demand for ethanol would increase the amount of land dedicated to corn production. And that would mean more water pollution, less water for other uses, and more ecosystem destruction.

In short, then, ethanol promises to reduce greenhouse gas emissions, but not by very much and at an unacceptable cost since there are any number of less expensive means to the same end. To add to the insult, ethanol worsens air and water quality and contributes to habitat destruction.

The rationales offered for the subsidies are useful narratives designed to convince non-farmers to embrace a program that will make them poorer so that some farmers can be richer.

Ethanol and Rural Economic Revitalization

While all of these arguments are made to justify ethanol subsidies, it's clear that the main reason the program has support in Washington is because ethanol subsidies increase corn prices and thus, farm and corn-processor income. The program concentrates great benefits on a few but diffuses costs to the many—the classic recipe for interest-group-driven government initiatives.

The rationales offered for the subsidies are useful narratives designed to convince non-farmers to embrace a program that will make them poorer so that some farmers can be richer. The highest-minded hope is that the subsidies will do something to reverse the long-term economic decline that has plagued rural towns and farms since the mechanization of agriculture in the late 19th century.

But as a morally uplifting project, ethanol gets poor grades. For starters, the belief that the transfer of wealth from non-farmers to farmers is progressive is not supported by the data. U.S. farm households earn about 11 percent more on average than non-farm households, and there is no particular reason to believe that the primary beneficiaries of more farm largesse would go to the poorest of those who still work the land.

And even if redistribution from the relatively poor to the relatively rich is something that political majorities wish to engage in, direct transfer payments would be preferable to the indirect transfer payments that follow from the ethanol program. That's because ethanol subsidies generate collateral damage. For instance, while rising corn prices (which are expected to go up 50 percent in 2007, due largely to the federal ethanol mandate) certainly help corn farmers, they hurt poultry, hog and cattle farmers, who rely on corn feed for their livestock. Increases in market demand for ethanol likewise help those who own ethanol-processing facilities, but harm soybean farmers, because many of the derivative products associated with ethanol production (like high-protein animal feed) compete in markets once dominated by soybean producers. In short, ethanol subsidies help some agribusinesses but hurt others.

Subsidy proponents also frequently overlook the fact the benefits bestowed by rising corn prices are capitalized into land values, and thus the wealth transfers associated with ethanol subsidies are almost completely captured by incumbent landowners. Accordingly, those who wish to enter into or expand in the farming business by buying or renting land will find that the subsidies provide little benefit to them. Note, too, that the more land one owns, the larger one's share of the federal subsidy will be—which highlights the truly regressive nature of the ethanol subsidy program.

Whether rural America witnesses a net increase in jobs as a consequence of the subsidies is almost immaterial from an economic perspective. After all, if the metric by which we were to judge public policy was the impact that a specific program might have on jobs in one narrow but favored slice of the economy, then banning all mechanized farm equipment and prohibiting farm imports would create far more jobs in rural America than is created by ethanol subsidies. No sane person would advocate turning back the clock in this way—unless, of course, rural job creation were to trump all other considerations.

Subsidies and Market Transformation

Would long-term, government subsidies trigger technological and organizational gains that transform the ethanol industry into a more productive enterprise, capable of delivering fuel at competitive prices? Subsidy proponents point to the Brazilian experience, where ethanol fuels have a big chunk of the market, as evidence of the miracle to be had.

A close examination of Brazil's ethanol market, however, reveals that major subsidies still persist and that ethanol there (made from sugar cane rather than corn) almost certainly couldn't compete in the market without government support.

Brazil's ethanol program was launched in 1975, when its dictator, Gen. Ernesto Geisel, ordered the country's gasoline to be mixed with 10 percent ethanol. That requirement was increased to 25 percent over the next five years and, under democratically elected governments, it has since varied between 20 and 26 percent. Generous subsidies were initially provided to sugar cane growers and ethanol processors, as well as to car manufacturers who built vehicles that could run on significant concentrations of ethanol fuels. But the oil price collapse of 1986 led the government to cut back on some of the most financially burdensome of those subsidies.

At present, Brazil provides a liberal tax subsidy to hydrous-ethanol producers (fuel that is about 95 percent ethanol and 5 percent water) and manufacturers who produce vehicles that can run on high-ethanol fuel blends. The government also imposes a national ban on competing diesel-powered cars (whose fuel costs are substantially below the cost of 25 percent sugar-cane fuel), maintains a federal alcohol-storage program to subsidize inventory holdings, and enforces a 21.5 percent import duty on foreign ethanol.

As a consequence, ethanol's share of the Brazilian motor vehicle fuels market has ranged between 40 and 55 percent since the mid-1980s. It's impossible to say, however, what the market share for ethanol might be without government-mandated use and other forms of assistance. The fact that Brazil was importing ethanol even with a steep import duty in place as late as January 2001—and from the United States no less!—suggests that the marginal production cost of sugar ethanol may be substantially higher than that of American corn ethanol.

In short, Brazil's subsidy program worked if we define "worked" as creating a significant market. It probably has not worked, however, if we define it as creating an industry that could compete without government help.

The American experience has been no better. Two economists, Richard Duke (McKinsey) and Daniel Kammen (University of California at Berkeley), constructed a model in 1999 to compare the benefits and costs of various federal market-transformation programs. While they found some evidence for the proposition that subsidies might help uneconomic industries become economically competitive in some cases, they found that federal ethanol subsidies have provided no net economic benefit despite more than 20 years of hand-holding.

"The ethanol market would collapse without the federal subsidy," they found, and additional subsidies were unlikely to improve matters because there are virtually no economies of scale associated with ethanol processing, production costs have declined only glacially over time, and ethanol production is a very mature technology. "It is therefore difficult to imagine a scenario," they conclude, "under which continuing the ethanol program can yield" a net gain to the economy.

Corn ethanol is more a religion than a reasoned proposition.

The Big Picture

Thus far, we have confined our discussion to corn and sugar cane ethanol. But what about cellulosic ethanol? The former uses the fruit of the plants in question, where a greater portion of the energy content is concentrated. The latter uses all of the plant's biomass—stalks, leaves, everything—to produce ethanol, and is the great long-term hope of ethanol proponents. Congress mandated that hope into law: the 2005 Energy Policy Act requires refiners to use 250 million gallons of cellulosic ethanol a year, starting in 2012.

The prospects aren't attractive, however, because the production costs of cellulosic ethanol are even higher than the costs of making alcohol from the fruit of the plant, and are likely to remain higher. With only a handful of cellulosic ethanol production facilities in the world, the Department of Energy's best guess is that cellulosic ethanol probably costs about $3.35 a gallon to produce at present. If all goes well, that might drop to $2.43 per gallon by 2020.

Cellulosic ethanol is, in theory, more attractive than corn ethanol because many of the plants we might harvest for processing require less fertilizer, pesticide and irrigated water to produce than corn does. Unfortunately, though, the energy yields are also significantly lower. Accordingly, even if production costs come down, cellulosic ethanol is unlikely to ever contribute more than a trivial amount to the transportation fuels market.

Of course, what the future holds for technology is unknowable. Perhaps scientists will engineer energy-intensive crops that can be harvested and processed at minimal cost. If that were to happen, we would have no complaint. But subsidies for existing technologies are unlikely to hasten that sort of market transformation and have been economically and environmentally counterproductive.

One might be tempted to cite the invasion of Wall Street into the ethanol industry as evidence that smart people with a lot of money are willing to bet to the contrary. But there is a better explanation: many ethanol investments make perfect sense in light of existing mandates to use the stuff and the lavish subsidies available to distill it. Without government favoritism, it's unlikely that investment would be more than a tiny fraction of its present level. In short, people are investing based on the politics of ethanol subsidies, not the economics of ethanol production.

Corn ethanol, as we noted at the outset, is more a religion than a reasoned proposition. People are entitled to their religious beliefs. But there ought to be a steep wall between church and state.

Organizations to Contact

The editors have compiled the following list of organizations concerned with the issues debated in this book. The descriptions are derived from materials provided by the organizations. All have publications or information available for interested readers. The list was compiled on the date of publication of the present volume; the information provided here may change. Be aware that many organizations take several weeks or longer to respond to inquiries, so allow as much time as possible.

American Coalition for Ethanol (ACE)
5000 South Broadband Lane, Suite 224
Sioux Falls, SD   57108
(605) 334-3381
Web site: www.ethanol.org

ACE is a nonprofit organization dedicated to increasing use and production of ethanol in the United States and to raising public awareness about the uses and benefits of ethanol. The organization serves as a clearinghouse for press releases, position papers, and research reports that are favorable to the ethanol industry. ACE publishes the monthly online magazine *Ethanol Today*, available online at www.ethanoltoday.com.

American Petroleum Institute (API)
1220 L Street NW, Washington, DC   20005-4070
(202) 682-8000
Web site: www.api.org

API is a trade organization representing America's oil and natural gas industries, advocating on behalf of its members before federal and state governments and the media. The organization funds research on all aspects of the petroleum industry, promulgates standards, and certifies the equipment used in producing oil and natural gas. API distributes more than 200,000 publications each year.

The Brookings Institution
1775 Massachusetts Avenue NW, Washington, DC 20036
(202) 797-6000
Web site: www.brookings.edu

The Brookings Institution is a nonprofit public-policy organization that produces research on a wide variety of public-policy issues and provides practical recommendations based on that research. The institution publishes books and journals written by its own researchers and by other authors on many policy-related topics, including a number of papers and opinion pieces on energy independence and climate change.

Cato Institute
1000 Massachusetts Avenue NW
Washington, DC 20001-5403
(202) 842-0200
Web site: www.cato.org

The Cato Institute is a conservative nonprofit public-policy research foundation dedicated to increasing the understanding of public policies based on the principles of limited government, free markets, individual liberty, and peace. The institute funds research on a wide variety of issues, provides free online subscriptions to articles on many topics, and annually awards the Milton Friedman Prize for Advancing Liberty.

The Institute for Local Self-Reliance (ILSR)
927 15th Street NW, 4th Floor, Washington, DC 20005
(202) 898-1610
Web site: www.ilsr.org

ILSR is a nonprofit organization that provides information and strategies to support environmentally sound and equitable community development. Issues of importance to the institute include efficient use of natural and financial resources, reduction of waste, and local ownership and control. ILSR has an ongoing project devoted to the carbohydrate economy, which publicizes such pieces as "The New Ethanol Future Demands a New Public Policy."

National Conference of State Legislatures (NCSL)
444 North Capitol Street NW, Suite 515
Washington, DC   20001
(202) 624-5400
Web site: www.ncsl.org

NCSL is a bipartisan organization that serves the legislators and staffs of the nation's 50 states, its commonwealths, and territories. NCSL provides research, technical assistance, and opportunities for policy makers to exchange ideas on pressing state issues. The organization provides an online bookstore and publishes the monthly magazine *State Legislatures*.

National Corn Growers Association (NCGA)
122 C Street NW, Suite 510, Washington, DC   20001
(202) 628-7001
Web Site: www.ncga.com

NCGA is the largest trade organization representing U.S. corn growers; it works to advance the interests of its members on issues of federal and state agricultural policies. The organization publishes position pieces and technical information on the corn industry and provides links to articles of interest to its members. NCGA also publishes a weekly newsletter called *Corn Commentary*.

Renewable Fuels Association (RFA)
One Massachusetts Avenue NW, Suite 820
Washington, DC   20001
(202) 289-3835
Web site: www.ethanolrfa.org

RFA is the primary lobbying organization for the American ethanol industry and works to promote governmental policies and regulations that encourage expanded use of ethanol and to provide information and research data about ethanol to its members and to the public. The RFA's Web site provides links to current news articles of interest to its members as well as to policy papers and issue briefs, such as "The Federal Ethanol Program: A Backgrounder."

Taxpayers for Common Sense (TCS)
651 Pennsylvania Avenue SE, Washington, DC   20003
1-800-TAXPAYER
Web site: www.taxpayer.net

TCS is a nonpartisan budget watchdog organization whose aim is to ensure that government spends tax dollars responsibly and operates within its means. The organization is known for identifying earmarks and wasteful spending in the federal budget and bringing them to the public's attention. TCS provides links to articles on all manner of government spending and denotes a section of its Web site to agricultural spending and subsidies in particular.

United States Department of Agriculture
1400 Independence Avenue SW, Washington, DC   20250
Web site: www.usda.gov

The Department of Agriculture is the federal agency charged with enacting the government's policies and regulations concerning food, agriculture, and related industries. The agency's Web site provides links to a variety of publications including policy statements, research reports, and fact sheets.

United States Department of Energy
1000 Independence Avenue SW, Washington, DC   20585
1-800-dial-DOE
Web site: www.energy.gov

The Department of Energy is the federal agency charged with enacting the government's directives and policies concerning energy, energy security, and the environmental cleanup of the nation's nuclear weapons complex. The agency provides up-to-date information on the current administration's energy policy and maintains a Web site specifically devoted to ethanol at www.afdc.energy.gov/afdc/ethanol.

Bibliography

Books

Albert Bates — *The Post-Petroleum Survival Guide and Cookbook: Recipes for Changing Times.* Gabriola Island, British Columbia: New Society Publishers, 2006.

David Blume — *Alcohol Can Be a Gas: Fueling an Ethanol Revolution for the 21st Century.* Santa Cruz, CA: International Institute for Ecological Agriculture, 2007.

Terry Boudreaux — *Ethanol and Biodiesel: What You Need to Know.* Houston, TX: Hart Energy, 2007.

Robert Bryce — *Gusher of Lies: The Dangerous Delusions of "Energy Independence."* New York: Basic Books, 2008.

Wendy Fernstrum — *High Octane: How Minnesota Led the Nation in Ethanol Development.* Shakopee: Minnesota Corn Growers Association, 2007.

S. David Freeman — *Winning Our Energy Independence: An Energy Insider Shows How.* Layton, UT: Gibbs Smith, 2007.